Wildlife
Photographer
of the Year
Portfolio 20

Lincolnshire
COUNTY COUNCIL

COMMUNITIESULTURAL SERVICES
and ADT EDUCATION

**This book shoule returned on or before
the last shown below.** SA

SAL 11/10		SA
18-5-11		
31-5-11		
27/3/2019		

To renew or order s please telephone 01522 782010
o ncolnshire.gov.uk
You will re onal Identification Number.
A er of staff for this.

Wildlife Photographer of the Year

Portfolio 20

Published by the Natural History Museum, London

First published by the Natural History Museum,
Cromwell Road, London SW7 5BD
© Natural History Museum, London, 2010
Photography © the individual photographers 2010

ISBN 978-0-565-09277-1

A catalogue record for this book is available from the
British Library.

Editor Rosamund Kidman Cox
Designer Bobby Birchall, Bobby&Co Design
Caption writers Rachel Ashton and Tamsin Constable
Colour reproduction and printing
Butler, Tanner and Dennis

Contents

Foreword

I am excited to hear that Spain's Altamira Cave – the Sistine Chapel of palaeolithic art – may be reopened to visitors. I want to go deep inside the dark cavern, admire face to face the extinct bison and feel the presence of those early artists.

With the eye of a painter, hunter and conservationist, I have viewed cave art in the Americas and Africa and have wondered about the representation of animals on these ancient walls and the vision of their creators. These men and women were more than painters: they were shamans – in essence, communal healers – with a rare capacity to change the perception of reality.

Like shamans, the best nature photographers use their skills for a purpose. They have seen the diversity, the beauty and the drama of the natural world but also witnessed first-hand the increasing loss of wilderness and biodiversity. Over time, this fuels a desire to 'heal nature' and to open the eyes of our communities.

Every year for the past 16 years, I have eagerly awaited the results of the Wildlife Photographer of the Year competition. I have never been disappointed. The collection of what now amounts to 20 books is extraordinary. They allow us to see thousands of photographs that capture unique moments and provocative visions.

London's Natural History Museum serves as the temple where this worship begins. In collaboration with hundreds of galleries and museums, the competition images are displayed to societies all over the world in what is the modern equivalent of the caves at Lascaux, Pintada or Altamira.

With the exhibitions and coverage by books, magazines, the internet and other media, this brilliant initiative reaches millions of people, communicating one message: wild nature is our best ally in tackling Earth's environmental problems.

Imagine the impact that the cave paintings had on the minds of young initiate shamans. Imagine them walking into the darkness of a cave and seeing, for the first time and in the dim light of flames, the images of rhinoceroses and cave bears. I believe the competition has had a similar impact on the visual imagination of young people.

Indeed, as a judge of this year's competition, it was the power of the vision of the younger generation of photographers that I found particularly inspiring. Their pictures were stunning – some even surpassing those of their older peers. What an initiation!

I strongly believe that this new generation of nature photographers will become effective warriors in the environmental battles. We need them. In the future, people will look at these photographs with curiosity and with anger at all the vanished species and wild places lost. And they will point their fingers at our generation.

But change can happen. Hand in hand, artists and natural scientists can help create a new era in which humankind reviews its values and re-encounters its natural roots. And the shamans among nature photographers have the skills to be at the forefront of this movement.

PATRICIO ROBLES GIL
Wildlife Photographer of the Year judge, photographer and President of Unidos para la Conservación, Mexico

The competition

Displayed in this book are all winning and commended images from the 2010 Wildlife Photographer of the Year competition, sponsored by Veolia Environnement. A showcase for the very best photography featuring natural subjects, the competition is owned by two UK institutions that pride themselves on revealing and championing the diversity of life: the Natural History Museum and *BBC Wildlife* Magazine. This year, the collection represents the work of 89 photographers from 25 countries.

Being placed in this competition, whether as commended or as a prize-winner, is something that wildlife photographers worldwide aspire to. Many of the chosen pictures are by professionals, but amateurs are well represented, too. That's because taking a winning picture of a natural subject is down to a mixture of vision, camera literacy, knowledge of nature – and luck. And this mixture doesn't necessarily require the latest equipment or a trip to an exotic location, as many of the shots by young photographers reveal. But it does require an eye for a picture.

The international panel of judges, representing professionals from other media as well as photography, look for pictures with that creative, original element that takes them beyond just representations of nature. Digital manipulation is not allowed; the welfare of the subjects is considered paramount; and wild and free conditions are championed.

The competition aims are

- to use its collection of inspirational photographs to make people, worldwide, wonder at the splendour, drama and variety of life on Earth;
- to inspire a new generation of photographic artists to produce visionary and expressive interpretations of nature;
- to be the world's most respected forum for wildlife photographic art, showcasing the very best images of nature to a worldwide audience;
- to raise the status of photography of wildlife into that of mainstream art.

The origins of the competition go back to 1964, when the magazine was called *Animals* and there were just 3 categories and about 600 entries. In 1981, it evolved into the form it takes now, and in 1984, *BBC Wildlife* Magazine and the Natural History Museum joined forces to create the international event it is today.

Now there are upwards of 30,000 entries (31,152 from 81 countries this year), a major exhibition at the Natural History Museum and exhibitions touring in the UK and around the world, from the Americas through Europe and across to the Far East and Australasia. The pictures appear in *BBC Wildlife* Magazine and publications worldwide. As a result, they are seen by many millions of people.

The judges

Mark Carwardine (Chair)
zoologist, writer, photographer
and conservationist

Richard Edwards
Director of Wildscreen's ARKive initiative

Colin Finlay
Head of Image Resources,
Natural History Museum, London

Daisy Gilardini
nature photographer

Rosamund Kidman Cox
editor and writer

Doug Perrine
marine photographer

Patricio Robles Gil
conservationist and photographer

Sophie Stafford
Editor, *BBC Wildlife* Magazine

Stefano Unterthiner
wildlife photographer

Solvin Zankl
wildlife photographer

The organizers

The competition is owned by the Natural History Museum
and *BBC Wildlife Magazine*, and is sponsored by Veolia Environnement.

Open to visitors since 1881, the Natural History Museum looks after a world-class collection of 70 million specimens. It is also a leading scientific research institution, with ground-breaking projects in more than 68 countries. About 300 scientists work at the Museum, researching the valuable collection to better understand life on Earth, its ecosystems and the threats it faces.

Last year, more than four million visitors were welcomed through the Museum's doors to enjoy the many galleries and exhibitions that celebrate the beauty and meaning of the natural world, encouraging us to see the environment around us with new eyes.

Wildlife Photographer of the Year is one of the Museum's most successful and long-running exhibitions. Together with *BBC Wildlife Magazine*, the Museum has made it the most prestigious, innovative photographic competition of its kind and an international leader in the artistic representation of the natural world.

The annual exhibition of award-winning images continues to raise the bar of wildlife photography and excite its loyal fans, as well as a growing new audience. People come to the Museum and tour venues across the UK and around the world to see the photographs and gain an insight into the diversity of the natural world – an issue at the heart of our work.

Visit www.nhm.ac.uk for what's on at the Museum.
You can also call +44 (0)20 7942 5000,
email information@nhm.ac.uk
or write to us at:
Information Enquiries
Natural History Museum
Cromwell Road
London SW7 5BD

For more than 45 years, the magazine has showcased the wonder and beauty of planet Earth, its animals and wild places – and highlighted its fragility.

By helping our community of more than 300,000 readers to understand, experience and enjoy the wildlife both close to home and abroad, we inspire them to care about the future of the natural world and take action to conserve it.

Every month, *BBC Wildlife* brings a world of wildlife to people's living rooms. We pride ourselves on our spectacular photography, and for this we rely on the photographers whose brilliance has been celebrated by the Wildlife Photographer of the Year competition since its launch in 1964.

Each issue includes page after page of beautiful photographs by the award-winning photographers – complete with the wild animals and even wilder stories behind them – and through their eyes we see the world's wildlife in all its glory.

You can take home all the winning images from the Wildlife Photographer of the Year 2010 competition in our exhibition guide, free with our November issue.

Visit www.bbcwildlifemagazine.com to subscribe
or find out more about *BBC Wildlife*.
You can also call +44 (0)117 927 9009
or email wildlifemagazine@bbcmagazines.com

We are extremely proud to be title sponsor of the Veolia Environnement Wildlife Photographer of the Year competition for the second year running.

Providing the right environmental services is our core business, and preserving natural habitats and animal species is essential to our present and future. The competition embodies the corporate values held by our company, such as our commitment to sustainable development, the preservation of natural resources and the very real need to inspire people of all ages.

This competition features the best of wildlife photography from across the world, highlighting the richness and diversity of nature, which is our responsibility to protect.

Jean-Dominique Mallet
Chief Executive Officer
Veolia Environmental Services (UK) Plc
www.veolia.co.uk

The Veolia Environnement
Wildlife Photographer of the Year Award

The Veolia Environnement
Wildlife Photographer of the Year

The Veolia Environnement Wildlife Photographer of the Year Award goes to Bence Máté, whose picture has been chosen as the most striking and memorable of all the entries in the competition.

Bence Máté

Bence was brought up in Pusztaszer, Hungary – one of the most significant migratory and nesting areas in Europe – and has been passionate about nature since a young age. He built his first hide at the age of 14, taking pictures using a borrowed camera and then saving enough money from breeding rabbits to buy his own equipment. At the age of 17, Bence won the Young Wildlife Photographer of the Year Award. Two years later he won the Eric Hosking Award, which he won again in 2007 and has won for the third time this year (see p132). He has also twice been made the Hungarian Nature Photographer of the Year.

A marvel of ants

Bence was determined to photograph leaf-cutter ants at work. But, where he was in Costa Rica, they seemed to do most of their cutting up in the trees. One night, after following columns of *Atta* ants for several hours, Bence found a smaller 'branch line' running up into a low-growing shrub, where they were cutting away.

As he tried to work out how to photograph the action, his head-torch beam fell on the underside of a leaf, silhouetting the ants on top. 'I could see all the behaviours all at once,' he says. 'The larger workers were hard at work cutting and carrying, while the smaller ones stood around on lookout,' probably for parasitic flies, which lay their eggs on the ants. Giant soldier ants guarded the trail.

He rushed to set up his beam behind the leaf, directed towards a tiny hole that the first leaf-cutters had already chopped out. By the time he was on the ground with his camera, the hole had grown. A few minutes later, the beam itself was visible through the hole. Bence had to keep getting up to reposition the lights. 'It was exhausting – I couldn't believe how fast they worked.' Within 20 minutes, the leaf-cutters had gone, taking their harvest back to the nest, where they would chew it, compost it and cultivate fungus on it to eat.

Creative Visions of Nature

This category is for conceptual pictures – original and surprising views of nature, whether figurative, abstract or ambiguous – which are judged purely on their artistic merits.

Nature's canvas

WINNER

Francisco Mingorance

SPAIN

Natural acidity and hundreds of years of mining have created this canvas – the famous 'painted river', the Rio Tinto, in Andalusia, Spain. Mineral ores (especially iron ore) oxidize when they come into contact with the air, staining the water and the land shades of red, orange and brown. Francisco has devoted more than 25 years to photographing the river, walking its length, diving in it, flying over it and exploring the mines. He took this aerial image of its copper-tinted waters from 500 metres (1640 feet) above the ground. It's a sight that he considers to be the perfect fusion of art and nature. 'I had to measure light, adjust the camera settings and compose images in fractions of a second, all the while fighting nausea and clinging to my camera in the strong wind.' The extraterrestrial impression may not be just artistic licence: astrobiologists think that the bacteria here live in conditions similar to those found on Mars.

Nikon D3 + 70-200mm lens; 1/3200 sec at f4.5; ISO 400.

The magical forest

RUNNER-UP

Sandra Bartocha

GERMANY

Gespensterwald (ghostly forest) is an old beech forest near Nienhagen,
Germany. It is buffeted by winds from the Baltic Sea, and these have
contributed to the lack of ground cover and the forest's reputation as a spooky
place. For Sandra, however, the forest is 'utterly beautiful'. After a heavy
snowfall in January, she spent the day alone in the forest. 'It was so silent,' she
says, 'that I could hear my heart pounding.' But it was only when it started to
get dark and the snow began to fall again that she had the chance to create
the surreal composition she hoped for, with the trees disappearing into snow
and a curtain of large, magical flakes falling in the foreground.

Nikon D700 + 24-70mm f2.8 lens; 0.8 sec at f5.6; ISO 200; internal flash.

Paradise performance

SPECIALLY COMMENDED

Tim Laman

USA

Tim has a passion for birds of paradise, and in the lowland forest at the base of the Arfak Mountains of West Papua, Indonesia, he set out to photograph the king bird of paradise. Having identified the most promising male and his vine-covered display tree, Tim built a platform in a tree opposite it and waited. The king tries to interest potential mates by showing off his spectacular plumage, often hanging upside down, jigging his tail wires so the iridescent-green discs flash above him. 'What I really wanted,' Tim says, 'was to highlight his distinctive features, especially those tail wires and his blue legs contrasting with his brilliant red body.' And that's the prize-winning composition he got.

Canon EOS 5D Mark II + 600mm f4 lens; 1/180 sec at f5.6; ISO 800.

Air display

HIGHLY COMMENDED

Andrew Parkinson
UNITED KINGDOM

Andrew's goal was to create a picture that would give something of the feeling of being at a gannet colony at the height of the breeding season – one of the great spectacles that the UK has to offer. Hermaness National Nature Reserve in the Shetland Islands was his chosen location, but to get a clear view of the colony, he had to scramble down about 20 metres (65 feet) of crumbling cliff face. Having reached a ledge, he then had to find enough space for his tripod and to steady it against the buffeting winds for the three-second exposure that would result in the effect he wanted.

Nikon D300 + 18-35mm lens + polarizing filter; 3 sec at f29; ISO 100; Gitzo tripod + Wimberley head.

Out of the blue

HIGHLY COMMENDED

Edwin Giesbers

THE NETHERLANDS

It was an overcast, drizzly summer day, but the mountain slopes near Malbun, Liechtenstein, were covered with flowers, and the lack of bright light was perfect for photography. Having found a particularly lovely clump of trumpet gentians, Edwin knelt down to take a closer look. 'As I peered into the flower, I saw several ants inside – a secret world you would never know existed until you look closely.' He spent some time trying to get the ants in focus, his task made more difficult because of the short depth of field and poor light conditions. Eventually, though, he decided on an abstract image. 'I love the way the ants seem to peer out at the world through a tiny little window.'

Nikon D300 + Tamron 90mm lens; 1/200 sec at f5.6; ISO 640.

Aerobatics

HIGHLY COMMENDED

Tanguy Stoecklé

FRANCE

Having observed and photographed yellow-winged bats for two years at
Lake Baringo, Kenya, Tanguy knows a lot about their behaviour and where they
roost and hunt. One of their favourite hunting spots is also one of the best for
photography – Tanguy's own camp, where they come some evenings to catch
insects attracted by the light. He regards them as among the most beautiful of
bats, with their golden wings and enormous golden ears, and was determined
to capture an impression of their action. After many nights, he achieved what
he was after, an impression of the beauty of the yellow-winged bat's aerobatics.

**Nikon D3 + 200mm lens; 1/80 sec at f5.6; ISO 1250; SB800 and SB26 flashes + manual
trigger; tripod.**

Lanzarote by moonlight

HIGHLY COMMENDED

Francisco Mingorance

SPAIN

Thirty million years ago, great slabs of the Earth's crust under the Atlantic Ocean fractured and crumpled up to create a vast underwater mountain range – the Mid-Atlantic Ridge. Colossal volcanoes followed, spewing up so much magma that, eventually, they poked up out of the sea to form the Canary Islands. Lanzarote, with more than 300 volcanoes, is Francisco's favourite. 'It has such a feeling of power, such a haunting beauty. The volcanic peaks, tubes and craters have been eroded by wind and rain to create a jagged landscape, full of surprising shapes and colours.' To create a sense of harmony, Francisco framed the lava spikes with a circle of star streaks around a constant North Star.

Nikon D3 + 24-70mm lens; 740 sec at f3.5; ISO 200.

Behaviour Mammals

In this category, the pictures are chosen for their action and interest value as well as for their aesthetic appeal.

The moment

WINNER

Bridgena Barnard

SOUTH AFRICA

'Today, as it's Christmas Day, we'll photograph a cheetah kill,' Bridgena announced to her family. They promptly fell about laughing. They had, after all, spent five days watching a trio of cheetahs in South Africa's Kgalagadi Transfrontier Park without seeing any activity. But Bridgena had discovered that the cheetah brothers had a favourite watch-out dune and a routine. By driving out at dawn to the spot, she hoped to be in position before rather than after any hunt. It was a good call. The cheetahs were positioned up on the dune, only the tops of their heads visible. When a trail of springbok passed by below, the brothers ignored the adults. But the moment a young springbok appeared, they sprinted after it, one heading it off, one tripping it up and the third making the kill. Within ten seconds it was over. The cheetahs had their meal and Bridgena had a phenomenal shot.

Nikon D700 + 500mm f4 lens + 1.7 converter; 1/4000 sec at f6.7; ISO 1600.

Red deer, blue haze

RUNNER-UP

Jean-Michel Lenoir

FRANCE

The red deer rut in the Ardennes Forest, France, is something that Jean-Michel has photographed over many years. On one afternoon, he watched a stag and his harem grazing peacefully in a wet meadow at the edge of the wood. When the light started to fade and the temperature fell, a mist started to rise up, creating a magical atmosphere. As he watched, Jean-Michel noticed a young stag crossing the meadow towards the group.
He knew that the harem owner would not tolerate the intruder and so focused on him. Tension rose. 'Then suddenly the big male charged. The chase across the meadow into the wood was incredibly fast, and the image captures exactly what I saw.'

Nikon F100 + 600mm f5.6 lens; 1/20 sec at f5.6; Provia 100F processed at 200; Gitzo tripod.

The thoughtful baboon

HIGHLY COMMENDED

Adrian Bailey

SOUTH AFRICA

Each morning, thousands of Cape turtle doves flock to a trickling seep at Mana Pools National Park, Zimbabwe, the only source of water for miles around. Birds of prey, meanwhile, line up in trees on nearby cliffs and pick off the drinking doves. Finding one of the victims on the ground close to the seep, and guessing it would be welcome booty for the chacma baboons already foraging nearby, Adrian set up his tripod in anticipation. This young male was the first to find the bird. 'He was almost circumspect, gazing at the body as though in deep thought,' says Adrian, 'unlike any other African carnivore, which would have been more likely to have grabbed the carcass and run off without a second thought.'

Nikon D2x + 500mm lens; 1/500 sec at f4; ISO 200; tripod.

Catch of the day

HIGHLY COMMENDED

Jordan Calame

USA

One unusually chilly morning, while walking along a deserted shoreline in Stump Pass State Park, Florida, Jordan spotted a single dorsal fin surfacing just offshore. Then more and more fins sliced the surface. Sprinting down the beach, camera in hand, he headed waist-deep into the icy surf. 'I stood in awe, with my finger fixed to the shutter release,' says Jordan, 'while a pod of seven dolphins chased their breakfast – yellow snappers. The dolphins came closer and closer until they were just feet away.' The spell was broken by the appearance of a fishing boat that drifted through them. The pod dispersed and Jordan headed back to his car to review his pictures, still in awe of his experience.

Canon EOS 40D + Tamron 28-300mm lens; 1/800 sec at f10; ISO 400.

A carcass-eye view

HIGHLY COMMENDED

Jürgen Ross

GERMANY

Fast, tall and with a kick that could shatter a lion's skull, adult giraffes usually have little to fear from predators. But in South Africa's Kruger National Park, one pride of lions has developed a shrewd hunting strategy. Jürgen explains: 'They pick out a giraffe and chase it towards a tarmac road. The giraffe struggles to run on the smooth surface, stumbles and falls.' It's a high-reward technique – a single giraffe feeds the lions for several days, as this one did. Here, a feeding lioness is framed by the carcass, through which she also keeps watch on the photographer.

Nikon D700 + 600mm f4 lens; 1/320 sec at f4.5; ISO 500; beanbag.

Lion and his little nipper

HIGHLY COMMENDED

Andrew Schoeman

SOUTH AFRICA

'Despite years in the bush, I have not seen many male lions who were tolerant of their cubs,' says Andrew. 'This male, however, was an exception.' His pride – 20 lionesses and their cubs – had spent the day asleep under an acacia tree in the Serengeti, Tanzania. He, meanwhile, had rested a distance away. Watching the cubs wake up and start to play, he began to walk over to join them. One cub ran out to meet him but then jumped at his hindquarters and sunk its claws in. The lion allowed the cub to hang on for a good few paces – giving Andrew the expressive shot he wanted – before finally snarling and shaking it off.

Canon EOS-1D Mark III + EF 100-400mm f4.5-5.6 lens; 1/13 sec at f10 (-1.3 e/w); ISO 100; beanbag.

Behaviour Birds

In this category, it's not enough for the picture to have aesthetic appeal. The subjects must also be doing something interesting or dramatic.

Snatch and grab

WINNER

Arto Juvonen

FINLAND

The fresh snow that covered the rubbish tip near Porvoo, on Finland's southern coast, didn't deter flocks of hungry crows, ravens and gulls searching for scraps. These scavengers, in turn, attracted goshawks, which perched hidden in the trees around the tip. Every so often, there would be panic among the scavengers as a goshawk suddenly swooped down and snatched a bird. Sometimes, the attack was from above, but always at great speed. For five winters Arto tried to capture the moment. 'I saw attacks many times, but something always prevented me from getting the shot I wanted.' In the end, though, his patience paid off. 'I love the clean background and the graceful wing curves,' he says. 'But every time I look at the image, I can hear the gull screaming.'

Canon EOS-1D Mark IV + 500mm f4 lens + 1.4x converter; 1/2500 sec at f7; ISO 1600.

The mobster

RUNNER-UP

Jim Neiger

USA

Jim has been photographing the birds on his home patch in Florida for a number of years and has got to know exactly where to find certain individuals, including a pair of great horned owls. One evening, just before sunset, he was focusing on one of the owls when a fish crow suddenly appeared above it and dived down, jabbing the owl with its feet. 'I got this image the instant before the crow made contact,' says Jim. 'The owl was obviously used to being mobbed. It barely flinched, shrugged off the crow and continued on its flight.'

Canon EOS-1D Mark III + 500mm f4 lens + 1.4x converter; 1/1000 sec at f5.6; ISO 1250.

Little owls on top

HIGHLY COMMENDED

Ilia Shalamaev

ISRAEL

In spring, the deserted quarry near the town of Kiryat Gat in Israel becomes a bird metropolis. Nest holes pepper the 20-metre-high (66-foot) walls, home to families of breeding bee-eaters, rollers and kestrels. This is where Ilia stationed his hide. Among the residents were a pair of little owls and their chicks. 'I noticed that the owls liked to perch on one particularly big rock,' he says. He dragged an even higher branch to the same spot, offering them a better vantage point in return for a sandy backdrop. The plan worked. Ilia then photographed the owls' domestic life to his heart's content, including tender moments such as this interaction between the three youngsters.

Canon EOS 5D + 500mm f4 lens + 1.4x converter; 1/250sec at f5.6; ISO 400; Gitzo tripod; hide.

Homage to stilts

SPECIALLY COMMENDED

Yossi Eshbol

ISRAEL

Black-winged stilts epitomize elegance, which helps explain why Yossi has been photographing them for more than 20 years. This picture is his all-time favourite, aesthetically but also because of the tender moment it shows. It was taken close to Yossi's home at salt ponds in Atlit. The stilts nest offshore, away from predators, building their nests out of salt crystals, which they scoop up from the bottom. As soon as the chicks hatch, they start feeding, looking for tiny crabs and other small water animals. Here the mother has called her newly hatched chicks back to the nest at sunset so they can dry out and warm up under her wings, alongside the egg she is still incubating.

Nikon D300 + 600mm f4 lens; 1/800 sec at f6.3 (-1.7 e/v); ISO 200; tripod; hide.

Pickings from puffins

HIGHLY COMMENDED

Marcello Calandrini

ITALY

It was the puffins in particular that Marcello had come to photograph on the Farne Islands, Northumberland, renowned for its breeding colonies of seabirds. 'I was busy photographing a group of puffins,' says Marcello, 'but sensed a commotion to one side' – a gaggle of black-headed gulls attempting to steal sand eels out of the beak of a returning puffin. Framing the scene in an instant, he pushed the shutter just once before the puffin escaped with its catch intact. 'Everything came together in that single moment,' he adds, 'action, composition, soft light and, most important, a pin-sharp puffin eye.'

Canon EOS-50D + EF 400mm f5.6 lens; 1/1000 sec at f5.6; ISO 500.

Sweet intimacy

HIGHLY COMMENDED

Christian Ziegler

GERMANY

At high altitudes, where there are few insect pollinators, orchids invite the services of hummingbirds with offers of nectar. This *Eleanthus* orchid, in a cloud forest in western Panama, was on the flower-patrol route of a male magnificent hummingbird, which would pass by every 40 minutes or so to check for freshly open florets. Whenever he dipped his beak in for a drink, a purple pollen package would stick to it, and he would inadvertently deliver this to the next orchid he visited. Christian captured the act in intimate detail by using a custom-made wide-angle macro lens, choosing an orchid that he could set up his camera next to and watching for two weeks, poised with cable-release in hand.

Canon EOS 5D Mark II + 17mm f2.8 lens; 1/60 sec; ISO 400; 6 flashes; remote trigger; tripod.

Behaviour
All Other Animals

This is a category for pictures of animals that are not mammals or birds – in other words, the majority of animals on Earth. Most of them behave in ways that are seldom witnessed and little known or understood. So this category offers plenty of scope for fascinating behaviour.

March of the crabs

WINNER

Pascal Kobeh

FRANCE

Each year, thousands of deep-sea Australian majid spider crabs set off to walk over the seabed to shallow waters off South Australia. In their drive to migrate, they climb over each other, sometimes forming great piles. 'They walked like an army on the march,' says Pascal. 'If I lay on the bottom, they would just clamber over me as though I was a lump of rock or coral.' Once in shallow water, many of them moult out of their exoskeletons (shells), emerging with soft new ones. It takes a while for the new, expanded shell to harden – a very vulnerable time for a crab. And this may be one reason for the great congregation: there is safety in numbers from predators such as rays. Great gatherings are also great places to find mates, and receptive females will attract large numbers of males. But aggregations don't always include receptive females, and males can't mate when they have soft shells. So the reason for the great migration is still partly a mystery.

Canon EOS-1Ds Mark II + 15mm lens; 1/60 sec at f9; ISO 400; Seacam housing.

Flight of the rays

RUNNER-UP

Florian Schulz

GERMANY

This astonishing aerial view of a massive
congregation of Munk's devil rays was taken
over the Sea of Cortez, Baja California, Mexico.
It's not unusual to see these smaller relatives
of the manta ray somersault out of the water –
locals call them tortillas because of the way they
slap down into the water. But as this wonderful
perspective shows, for all the individuals leaping
out that are visible at sea level, there are many
more below the surface. 'When I first saw this
wildlife phenomenon from the distance,' says
Florian, 'I was not sure what I was looking at.
The ocean was boiling. It was hard to tell how
many rays there were, because the shoal must
have been as thick as it was wide.' And this
image shows only a quarter of the whole scene –
Florian cropped the photo to emphasize just how
concentrated the rays were. No one knows why the
rays gather like this, whether to mate, herd prey or
migrate or just for the sheer joy of being together.

Nikon D3X + 200-400mm f4 lens; 1/800 sec at f4.5; ISO 800.

Behaviour All Other Animals

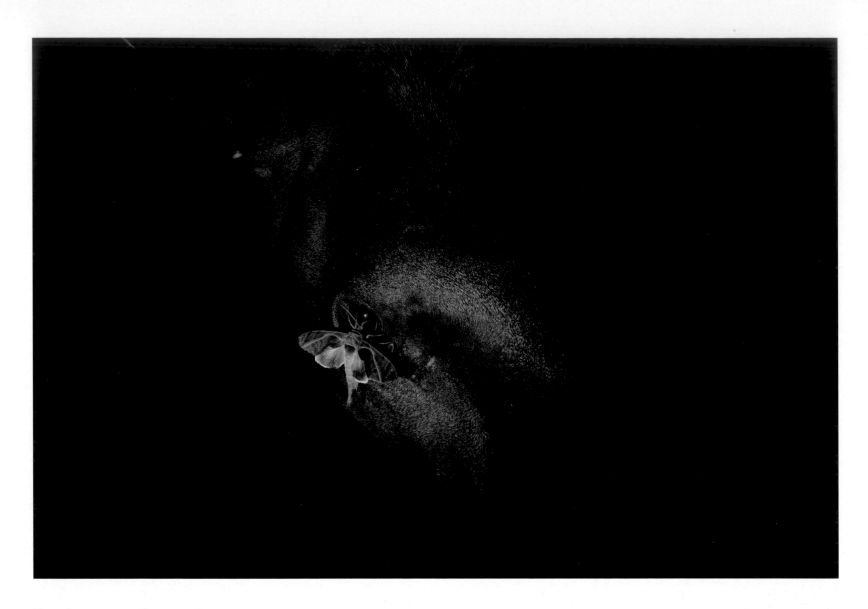

In the eye of a tapir
HIGHLY COMMENDED

David Herasimtschuk

USA

Many nights spent hiking to swamps and lakes in Ecuador in search of frogs (his research subject) have revealed to David countless new animals and behaviours. Particularly fascinating are the lachryphagous (eye-frequenting) moths. The tapir that this moth is drinking from had been rescued as a baby and released back into the wild. So it was used to humans and allowed David to follow it through the forest. 'Whenever it stopped to eat or rest,' he says, 'as many as five or six moths would settle around an eye.' These moths have evolved to feed on secretions from mammal eyes and, in this case, may even prefer to drink from the eyes of tapirs.

Canon EOS 5D + EF 17-40mm f4 lens; 1/40 sec at f13; ISO 400; Speedlite 580EX flash + transmitter ST-E2.

The ant-shepherd and its little flock

HIGHLY COMMENDED

Matt Cole

UNITED KINGDOM

Matt has often tried to photograph black garden ants milking black bean aphids in his garden. It's a common enough sight, but showing ants in the act (stroking the aphids with their feelers to encourage them to excrete drops of honeydew) and creating a composition that works is another matter. 'The ants rarely stand still for more than a second or two and tend to clamber over each other and the aphids.' Here, though, an ant stands still as if guarding its clutch, its antennae gently stroking the aphids. Watching insect behaviour through a macro lens has transformed Matt's photographic ambitions. 'I used to take portraits,' he says, 'but now I'm obsessed with insects and their activities.'

Canon 450D + MP-E 65mm lens; 1/160 sec at f10; ISO 100; Speedlite 580EXII diffused flash.

A miracle of monarchs

HIGHLY COMMENDED

Axel Gomille

GERMANY

Millions of monarch butterflies migrate down North America to spend the winter in the small, cold but sheltered forest site of El Rosario, high in the mountains of central Mexico. 'The sheer density is unbelievable,' says Axel. 'I had never seen anything like this before. It was breathtaking. They landed on my fingers, my cap, my camera – everywhere.' In March, as the temperature increases, the monarchs start to become more active and the migration northward begins. After warming up in the first rays of the early-morning sun, the roosting monarchs fly down to drink: they need water to make use of their tiny fat reserves. Axel's aim was to capture both the butterflies' movement and their rich colours 'lit up against the dark forest backdrop'. This required lying almost in the puddle, so that the sun lit the butterflies from the side, highlighting the ones in the air. 'When they take off, it sounds like wind.'

Nikon D300 + 17-55mm f2.8 lens at 17mm; 1/125 sec at f13; ISO 500.

Nature in Black and White

What pictures here must display is skilful and artistic use of the black-and-white medium. The subject can be any wild landscape or animal.

Storm gathering

WINNER

Antonio Busiello

ITALY

The giraffes were part of a group that Antonio had been following for several days in Tanzania's Lake Manyara National Park. They had spent the early morning browsing in wooded savannah but then began to drift away across the plain. When the storm clouds began to thicken, Antonio realized he had components that would express the essence of the African wilderness: an iconic wild animal, a vast space and a rolling, darkening sky. 'At one point, the giraffes stopped, as though waiting for the storm. It was a wonderful contrast between a quiet moment and a strong, dramatic event.' Shortly after, the clouds burst.

Nikon D3 + 70-200mm f2.8 lens; 1/125 sec at f22; ISO 320.

Emerging blackbuck

RUNNER-UP

Back in, front out

HIGHLY COMMENDED

Esa Mälkönen

FINLAND

It made perfect sense to photograph the comings and goings of the chinstraps in black and white. During his time at the penguin rookery on Deception Island in South Shetland, Antarctica, Esa became more and more fascinated with the activities of the 100,000 or so penguins. Having paired up, a male and female will devise a rota: one sits on the eggs (for up to five days) while the other walks back to the sea to feed. 'Even from a distance it was easy to see who was doing what. Black backs told one story, white fronts another,' says Esa. The challenge was to get a shot showing both the backs and fronts of the penguins in an arrangement that worked aesthetically – 'not too few and not too many'.

Canon EOS 7D + 300mm f2.8 lens; 1/2000 sec at f11; ISO 1600.

Desert survivor

HIGHLY COMMENDED

Morkel Erasmus

SOUTH AFRICA

It was a particularly quiet day in the Kalahari Desert, South Africa. 'The sky was streaked with wonderful cirrus clouds,' says Morkel, 'looking as if it had been swept with an invisible broom.' He couldn't believe his luck when a lone blue wildebeest wandered into the scene and posed against the dramatic backdrop. 'I wanted to celebrate the wildebeest as a desert survivor,' adds Morkel, 'caked in dust, constantly on the search for food and water, dodging the onslaught of predators.' It was noon, the light was harsh, and so black and white was a fitting medium to immortalise this moody scene.

Canon EOS 1000D + 18-55mm lens; 1/250 sec at f16; ISO 200.

Out of the ashes

HIGHLY COMMENDED

Britta Jaschinski

UNITED KINGDOM/GERMANY

Britta arrived in Ndutu, Tanzania, only days after a huge bushfire blazed through the area. 'Vast tracts of acacia trees were burnt to the ground, and the air reeked of ash and cinders,' says Britta. The scorched ground was dotted with whitened tortoise shells, and disorientated antelopes were wandering around with nowhere to hide – a windfall for predators. One evening, a cheetah appeared on the blackened scene. 'But it, too, looked unsettled, alienated – almost ghostly.' Britta took the photo using a long exposure to catch the mood of the moment and then watched as the cheetah melted into the background.

Nikon FE2 + 200mm fixed lens; 1/8 sec at f4; Kodak 400TX.

Tom Schandy

NORWAY

Tom was surrounded by about 20 European elk when he took this photograph.
His hide was his car, and the elk had arrived to eat the vegetables that farmers
put out for them every winter in the same spot, at Sylling near Oslo, Norway.
With so many so close, he could 'play with form and different perspectives.'
What particularly fascinated Tom about this female was her fur texture.
He used the snow-covered field as a backdrop, deliberately mimicking
the effect of a studio portrait.

Canon EOS-1D Mark III + EF 300mm f2.8 lens; 1/100 sec at f4; ISO 800.

Lookout

HIGHLY COMMENDED

Ken Dyball

AUSTRALIA

Ken had got to know this caracal well. Living in Kenya's Masai Mara, he was a young male, whose mother appeared to be trying to encourage him to become independent. 'She would leave him alone for long periods of time,' says Ken, 'presumably hoping he would learn to fend for himself. He slept in a den in the ground during the day, emerging in the evening to wait for her.' Early one morning, as Ken explored the spot where he had last seen the caracal, he heard the thunder of hooves. As a herd of wildebeest galloped past, pursued by hyenas, the terrified young caracal shot out of the grass and up the nearest tree. He did the right thing. 'They stampeded straight over his den,' says Ken.

Nikon D700 + 400mm f2.8 lens + 1.7 converter; 1/250 sec at f9; ISO 500; custom car mount + Manfrotto head.

In Praise of Plants

The aim of this category is to showcase the beauty and importance of flowering and non-flowering plants and fungi, whether by featuring them in close-up or as part of their environment. Without plants, there would be no animals.

Ephemeral gift

WINNER

Frédéric Demeuse

BELGIUM

Small and delicate, the fruiting bodies of this little bonnet fungus are hard to find, and it took a lot of searching through beech leaf-litter before Frédéric found a clump of the toadstools in Belgium's Sonian Forest. He set up his tripod and then waited for cloudy conditions that would give him the soft lighting he wanted. 'I made the tiniest toadstool the subject of the composition, positioning it so that its shape was echoed by the central big one behind – a projection of what it would look like very soon.' He describes the delicate group as 'a gift from nature'.

Nikon D300 + 105mm f2.8 lens; 1/10 sec at f5.6 (+ 0.3 e/v); ISO 250; tripod + Rotule ballhead + angle viewfinder + mirror-locked and ML-3 remote control.

Floodwater tapestry

RUNNER-UP

Peter Cairns

UNITED KINGDOM

The Insh Marshes National Nature Reserve in Scotland's Cairngorms National Park is one of Europe's most important wetlands. Each winter, its main artery, the River Spey, spills onto the floodplain, submerging the vegetation and providing a winter refuge for migratory wildfowl. 'I was initially attracted to this scene by the perfect reflection of the tree trunks in the still floodwater,' says Peter, 'but it was the subtle green of the lichens and the purple-tinged buds that made the scene so beautiful. Willow, alder and birch come together in a seemingly chaotic way but are underwritten by perfect ecological order.'

Canon EOS 5D Mark II + 70-200mm lens; 1/5 sec at f16; ISO 200; Gitzo tripod.

Chris Linder

USA

A treasured symbol of the American Southwest,
the saguaro cactus occurs only in southern
Arizona, northern Mexico and a small area of
California. It's the world's largest cactus, and yet
it is incredibly slow-growing, with a lifespan of
150 years or more. During its life, it provides
nectar and fruits as well as homes for numerous
desert animals, including woodpeckers and owls.
Chris set out to capture the grandeur of this
individual, growing in the Organ Pipe Cactus
National Monument, Arizona, and 'convey
the feeling of awe I felt while walking among
such giants.' To achieve the star-studded
background, he used a high ISO to keep the stars
from blurring and created the halo by positioning
the rising moon behind one of the saguaro's arms.

**Nikon D700 + 14-24mm f2.8 lens; 30 sec at f2.8; ISO 3200;
Gitzo GT3540LS tripod + Kirk ballhead.**

Bugloss at sunset

SPECIALLY COMMENDED

Francisco Mingorance

SPAIN

As the sun sets, a red bugloss points towards the emerging stars from its craggy foothold of volcanic rock. This spectacular plant is found only on Tenerife, one of the Canary Islands. Its massive floral spikes can reach up to 3 metres (10 feet) in height, giving it its other common name, the tower of jewels. Francisco included in the distance the silhouette of a famous Tenerife landmark, the Roques de García, to enhance the drama of the composition. 'There was no moon that night, so I had to rely on the fading dusk for light,' says Francisco. To track the stars, he exposed the shot for a full 20 minutes. 'I only had one chance before the light went,' he says. 'Luckily, the timing worked.'

Nikon D3 + 24-70mm lens; 983 sec at f5.6; ISO 200.

Grass strokes

HIGHLY COMMENDED

Georg Kantioler

ITALY

'I often search for simple motifs,' says Georg. 'I'm not interested in finding rare plants or animals. I like to show the quiet beauty of everyday subjects.'
The subject for this picture – delicate fox tail grass – was found one warm, sunny spring morning in dry grassland near his home in the South Tyrol, northern Italy. He took time experimenting with camera settings and angles 'to arrange the picture, sometimes changing my position by several centimetres, then by a matter of just a few millimetres,' varying the focus and then opening up the lens until he had the 'smooth pastel shades' and the 'tender, peaceful' picture he was after.

Canon EOS 5D Mark II + 100mm f2.8 lens; 1/30 sec at f3.2; ISO 200.

Orchid in a flush of garlic

HIGHLY COMMENDED

Sandra Bartocha

GERMANY

The scent of wild garlic wafted on the sea air as Sandra wandered through a meadow near the coastal town of Vieste, Italy. The field was a riot of colour, thick with Naples garlic and hundreds of pyramidal orchids. Invisible cicadas buzzed loudly, accompanied by the calls of bee-eaters. What Sandra wanted to conjure up was the brightness and freshness of the spring morning. Discovering a tall Apulian bee orchid, she photographed the flower against the sea, 'keeping the orchid in shadow but making use of the fantastic morning light bouncing off the glossy surfaces of the garlic and water' to create the sparkling setting.

Nikon D200 + 105mm f2.8 lens; 1/5000 sec at f3.3; ISO 100; reflector.

Flowers of the volcano

HIGHLY COMMENDED

Francisco Mingorance

SPAIN

Life among the sharp volcanic rocks of Tenerife's Teide National Park is tough. 'The Canary Islands' climatic isolation, together with 40 million years of physical isolation, has led to the evolution of unique species,' says Francisco. 'Volcanoes create a world in which everything is exceptional, virgin and wild.' The rare red bugloss is considered a floral treasure, symbolic of the exclusive wildlife of this mini-continent. Francisco spent many days looking for the right grouping of plants, finally discovering this tight clump of flowering spikes on the Ucanca plain. The Mount Teide volcano provided the perfect backdrop, and Francisco positioned his tripod so that the North Star would appear just above the crater.

Nikon D3 + 14-24mm f2.8 lens; 637 sec at f5; ISO 200.

Salt-desert cacti

HIGHLY COMMENDED

Jordi Busqué

SPAIN

Salar de Uyuni, Bolivia, is one of the more extraordinary places on the planet. At 3656 metres (11,995 feet) above sea level in the Andes, it's not only the world's largest salt pan, visible from outer space, but also one of the flattest places on Earth. Huge pasacana cacti grow there, some hundreds of years old and more than 10 metres (33 feet) high. 'I wanted to show just how vast, silent and otherworldly a place this is,' says Jordi. He chose to photograph them in the soft light of sunrise. A shimmer of water left over from the rainy season makes the small mountain seem to float on the horizon – a mountain that is made from fossilized coral, adding geological intrigue to the place.

Nikon D300 + 18-200mm VR lens; 1/125 sec at f11; ISO 200.

Animals in Their Environment

A winning photograph must create a sense of place and convey a feeling of the relationship between an animal and where it lives.

Sharp reflection

WINNER

Jochen Schlenker

GERMANY

Jochen went to the mountains of Aiguilles Rouges in the French Alps specifically to take photographs of ibex. These wild goats are high-altitude grazers, well adapted to the steep, rocky terrain of the Mont Blanc region. Having spent all afternoon taking photographs of ibex, Jochen set up his tripod to photograph the pin-sharp reflection of the jagged mountains in the smooth surface of the Lac des Chéserys. 'There were interesting cloud formations, and with no wind, the reflections were perfect,' says Jochen. 'Then a lone ibex walked by in the distance, completing the image.'

Nikon D300 + 16-85mm f3.5-5.6 lens + polarizer + 1-stop ND grad filter; 1/100 sec at f8; ISO 200; cable release; tripod.

Storm riders

RUNNER-UP

Ben Cranke

SOUTH AFRICA/UNITED KINGDOM

The Scotia Sea crossing to the Falkland Islands was a rough one, and the ship was battered by storms. Suffering from a bad bout of seasickness, Ben clambered on deck, determined to photograph the birds that had been tirelessly following the ship. 'Unlike us, they were completely at ease,' says Ben. 'I was in awe of them. They would bank when caught up in the headwinds, turn and begin the chase all over again.' At times the sky was full of birds, mostly Cape petrels. As the light faded, Ben anchored himself to the railings at the stern, leaning out to photograph the petrels riding the wind in the wake of the ship.

Nikon D3 + 24-70mm f2.8 lens; 1/1000 sec at f8; ISO 800.

Dawn call

HIGHLY COMMENDED

Pierre Vernay

FRANCE

The roar of a red deer stag carries an unmistakable message: the more powerful the roar, the stronger the stag. The sound is designed to carry in a forest, leaving both hinds and competitors in no doubt about the caller's physical superiority. To catch the action of the rut, Pierre stationed himself in Dyrehaven forest, an ancient deer park north of Copenhagen in Denmark. Going out at dawn, he planned to photograph the deer backlit against the rising sun. Just as the very first beams of sunshine lit up the grass, a stag emerged from below a huge oak tree to challenge a rival that had strayed too close. One set of bellowing was enough – the rival got the message, loud and clear, and vanished.

Nikon D3 + 500mm f4 lens; 1/640 sec at f6.3; ISO 800.

Snowed in

HIGHLY COMMENDED

Orsolya Haarberg

NORWAY / HUNGARY

Orsolya camped through winter storms in Norway's Dovre-Sunndalsfjella National Park to photograph muskoxen. On particularly cold days, muskoxen conserve energy by resting. It's then possible to approach them, but if you get too close and spook them, there is a real risk of being trampled. 'For two days,' says Orsolya, 'the wind was so strong and it snowed so much that I couldn't even see the animals.' But the next day it stopped snowing, and the massive forms of muskoxen emerged from the landscape. 'It was a unique scene, and I forgot about time and pain,' says Orsolya. 'But muskoxen had more stamina than I did. I lost the feeling in my hands and feet and so was forced to leave.'

Nikon D700 + 300mm f2.8 lens; 1/2000 sec at f5.6; ISO 400; Gitzo GT3540LS tripod.

The drop

HIGHLY COMMENDED

Andrew Parkinson

UNITED KINGDOM

With his legs dangling over the edge, Andrew tried to avoid any foreground showing in the picture by leaning right into the gale-force westerly blowing off the Atlantic. 'Like so many people with a fear of heights, I am almost hypnotically drawn to drops, and I was determined to show the fulmar as part of this spectacularly precipitous landscape – though if the wind had stopped, I might have had a problem.' The fulmar is such an aerodynamic bird that the splayed tail feathers and legs seem comically incongruous. But the bird was, in fact, coping perfectly well with the winds surging up the cliff face. Indeed, it seemed to be just enjoying riding the swells.

Nikon D300 + 18-70mm lens; 1/100 sec at f6.3; ISO 400.

Swamp heaven

HIGHLY COMMENDED

Mac Stone

USA

Mac spent months in the Francis Beidler Forest, South Carolina, photographing one of the world's largest stands of virgin cypress and tupelo trees. His aim was to show a positive view of swamps, so often regarded as worthless if not dangerous. In one lake he discovered a log that was a magnet for sunbathers. But the only way to get close enough to photograph the animals without disturbing them was to mount his camera on the log. He programmed it to take a picture every ten minutes. What it revealed was a constant stream of visitors, including this yellow-bellied slider and American alligator, in swamp heaven under the sun.

Canon EOS 50D + 10-22mm lens; 1/8 sec at f22; ISO 100; Manfrotto Magic Arm + Super Clamp; Canon Intervalometer.

Urban Wildlife

These pictures must show wild plants or animals in an urban or suburban environment, with the human presence being very much part of the picture.

Street-walker

HIGHLY COMMENDED

Chris O'Reilly

UNITED KINGDOM

The use of the car window was deliberate, as was framing the fox small, under lamplight – a street-walker spied on. He wanted to show a dog fox in its urban environment doing what a dog fox does at night: make his territorial rounds. The snow on the ground resulted in a freezing night in the car but acted as a reflector for the street lighting. Chris started photographing foxes on his home patch in Chellaston, Derby, nearly two years ago, when he realized that the improved sensitivity of his digital camera meant he could photograph in low light without flash. Now familiar with his local foxes, he can anticipate the time of arrival and behaviour of most of his street-walker subjects.

Canon EOS-1Ds Mark III + 16-35mm lens; 1/20 sec at f2.8; ISO 1600; cable-release; tripod.

Paris life

HIGHLY COMMENDED

Laurent Geslin

FRANCE

Laurent set out to photograph wildlife in the heart of Paris. He encountered kestrels, sparrowhawks and even kingfishers, but what proved to be the challenge was giving them a sense of place. When he discovered there were rabbits living in a park close to the Arc de Triomphe, he set out to photograph them after nightfall. He first shot them with the famous monument in the background. He then realized that there was a far more interesting cityscape right behind him – La Défense business area had the contemporary edge that he was looking for. Laurent got on his belly, and the rabbits obliged by keeping their ears up, silhouetted by the bright lights of modern Paris.

Nikon D3 + 70-200mm f2.8 VR lens; 1/5 sec at f6.3; ISO 800.

Cold comfort

HIGHLY COMMENDED

Michael Patrick O'Neill

USA/BRAZIL

In early January 2010, Florida was in the grip of an exceptionally cold snap. Manatees can't survive when water temperatures fall below 18°C (65°F), and in winter, many depend on warm river springs or, as here, cluster around the tepid water discharged from power plants along the coast. 'I chartered a helicopter,' says Michael, 'and used a wide-angle lens to reveal the industrial nature of the winter habitat of some of Florida's manatees,' in this case, Riviera Beach in Palm Beach County – a hugely important site for them. Such a concentration of these giant marine herbivores could make you think that the species isn't endangered. But it is. A record 430 died of cold that winter.

Nikon D2x + 16mm f2.8 lens; 1/1000 sec at f9; ISO 200.

Sunset moment

HIGHLY COMMENDED

Olivier Puccia

FRANCE

Squeezed out of their forest homes by deforestation and the spread of human habitation, Hanuman langurs have become part of urban life in many parts of India. Revering them as the reincarnation of their Hindu monkey-like deity Hanuman, locals often feed them. Olivier visited a hilltop temple – a Hanuman langur hotspot – overlooking Ramtek in Maharashtra, western India. As the sun began to set, he tried to find the highest point from which to admire the glorious scene. Just below, this mother and baby were wrapped in each other's arms, staring across the valley. 'It was a touching moment,' says Olivier, 'as though they were appreciating the sunset together.'

Canon EOS 5D Mark II + EF 16-35mm f2.8 lens; 1/160 sec at f3.5; ISO 200.

Wild Places

This is a category for landscape photographs but ones that convey a true feeling of wildness and create a sense of awe.

A wild wonder of Europe

WINNER

Maurizio Biancarelli

ITALY

After two days of torrential rain, Maurizio's luck changed. He was on assignment in Plitvice Lakes National Park, Croatia, a small but beautiful World Heritage Site – 'a real wild wonder of Europe' – with the goal of photographing the Veliki Prstvaci waterfalls. On the third day, arriving well before dawn, Maurizio saw for the first time the sun rise. 'Everything came together in the most serendipitous way,' he says. Gloriously soft light played through the mist and highlighted the lush tapestry of woodland colour. 'I especially like the dream-like quality of this image,' he adds. 'It's easy to forget that it was taken in Europe – a reminder of what a powerful tool photography can be.'

Nikon D3 + 24-70mm f2.8 lens; 1/4 sec at f11; ISO 200; Gitzo 3540 tripod.

Southern swell

RUNNER-UP

Kah Kit Yoong

AUSTRALIA

Hanson Bay on Kangaroo Island, South Australia, faces the Southern Ocean and the full force of its massive swells and storms, which blow in from Antarctica. 'The tide was too high for the first two shoots,' says Kah Kit, 'but on the third, at sunrise, there was a storm.' As the dawn light filtered through the dark clouds, the tide was low enough for him to stand on the rocks. But rain and sea spray were a huge problem. 'I had to keep wiping the lens and filters,' says Kah Kit. 'In fact, saltwater damage caused my camera body to stop working altogether after this shoot.' The slow shutter gave the ethereal effect he was after, as if the sea were draining away at the edge of the world.

Canon EOS-1Ds Mark III + 16-35mm f2.8 lens + Singh-Ray reverse-graduated neutral-density filter; 2.5 sec at f11; ISO 100; Gitzo Explorer tripod.

Rock art

SPECIALLY COMMENDED

Verena Popp-Hackner

AUSTRIA

For more than a month, Verena photographed the reptile-like ridges of sandstone on Norway's Varanger Peninsula in all weather conditions. 'Every time I went, a new combination of light, tide and weather made the seaweed-covered rocks look different,' she says. 'Some colours were stronger when the rock was wet. Others reflected indirect sunlight well. Others were better in shade.' Eventually, on a stormy day at high tide, everything came together. Balanced on a slippery ridge, Verena used a long exposure to soften the water as a contrast to the rocks. 'On this day, the colour combination was pure magic.'

Toyo Field 45 AII + Schneider 75mm f5.6 lens; 8 sec at f45; Fujichrome Velvia 50.

Celestial cathedral

HIGHLY COMMENDED

Kent Miklenda

AUSTRALIA

The aurora borealis – here taking place in the night sky over the Lofoten Islands, northern Norway – 'was a sublime experience,' says Kent, who shared the awe that our ancestors surely felt when observing the cosmic display. 'Standing under the brilliant roof of stars and shimmering curtains of light was evocative of being in a kind of celestial cathedral.' The natural physics behind the phenomenon is also impressive, involving atomic collisions of the solar winds and the Earth's magnetic field lines creating ionizing gases that flux and glow in the atmosphere.

Canon EOS-1Ds Mark III + 16-35mm f2.8 II lens; 38 sec at f2.8; ISO 400; Manfrotto 555B carbon tripod + levelling head + ballhead; Wimberley Arca-Swiss-style QR clamp; Kirk L-Bracket; Yongnuo radio-remote shutter release.

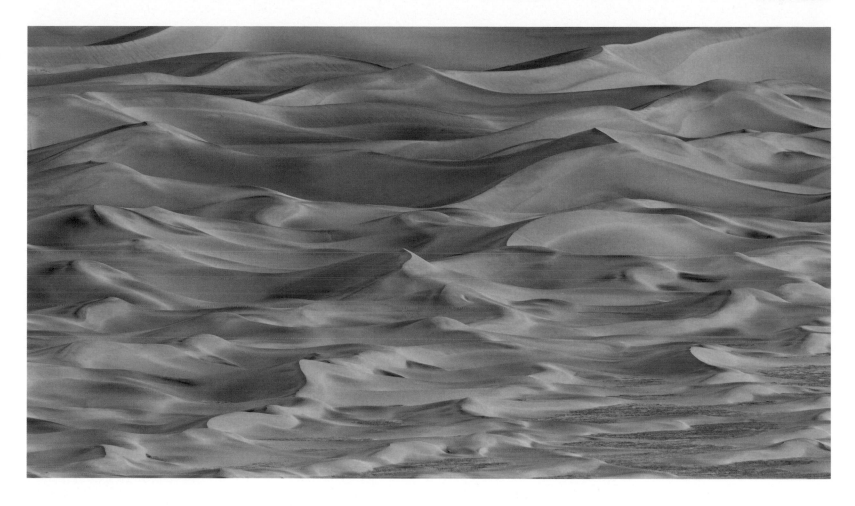

Death Valley dunes

HIGHLY COMMENDED

Floris van Breugel

USA/THE NETHERLANDS

Sunrise bathes the Mesquite Sand Dunes in California's Death Valley National Park in pinks and oranges and creates the shadows that emphasize the wind-whipped dunescapes. To avoid any detail and a sense of scale, Floris stationed himself a good distance away, overlooking the valley, and used a telephoto lens. 'The sensual forms and ever-changing nature of sand dunes fascinate me more than any other landscape,' he says.

Canon 5D Mark II + 500mm lens + 1.4x teleconverter; 5 sec at f4; ISO 100; Gitzo tripod + Markins ballhead + Wimberley sidekick.

Underwater World

The subjects in this category can be marine or freshwater species but must be featured under the water. The pictures themselves must be memorable, either because of the behaviour displayed or because of their aesthetic appeal – and, ideally, both.

The big four

WINNER

Tony Wu

USA

Tony spent an unforgettable morning snorkelling above a large group of sperm whales off the Caribbean island of Dominica. 'They spent much of their time at the surface of the ocean, rubbing up against each other, vocalizing and gathering in raft formations – often appearing as if they were playing,' says Tony. 'Though they were preoccupied, the whales seemed to take an interest in me from time to time.' When he took this photograph, four were swimming directly up towards him. They paused about 10 metres (33 feet) below the surface, and as Tony dived down to have a better look, he could feel their clicking sonar resonating through his body as they checked him out. Then suddenly they surfaced, and Tony found himself in the middle of the four enormous animals. 'As I swam along with them and we made eye contact, it seemed as if, however briefly, they were socializing with me.'

Canon EOS 5D Mark II + 15mm f2.8 fisheye lens; 1/400 sec at f4.5; ISO 200; Zillion housing.

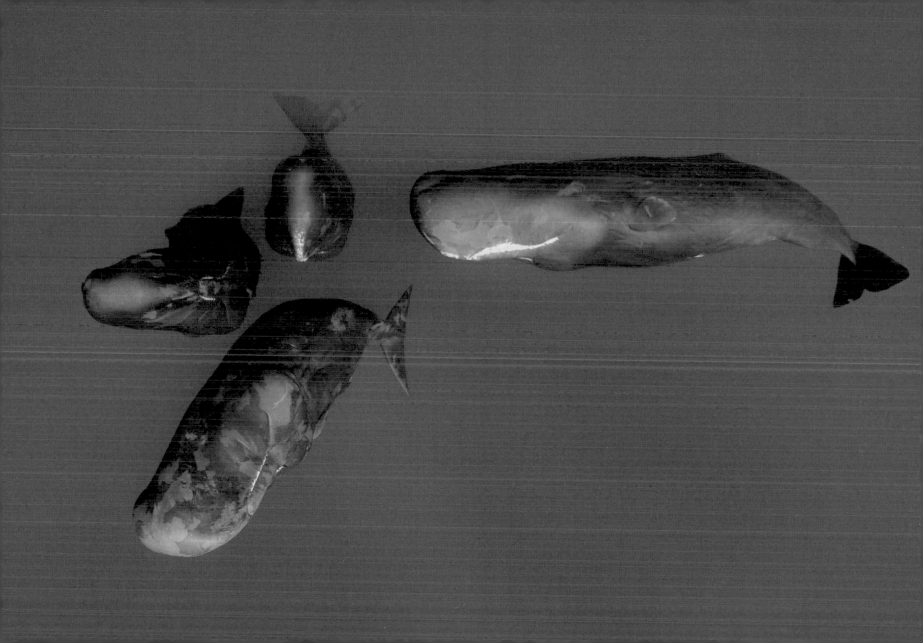

Bottom view

RUNNER-UP

Michel Roggo

SWITZERLAND

Michel is passionate about revealing the beauty of freshwater life and spends much of his time photographing below the surface. In winter, in calm parts of the River Rhine, Switzerland, fish gather in dense groups. 'I'd got an image in my head of a mass of motionless fish,' says Michel, 'chub, bream, sander ...' and that was the picture he set out to take. So when a mute swan swam into the frame and then a girl on the bridge above began dropping bits of bread onto the water to feed the chub and the swan, he was very frustrated. But then he realized that the swan's rear end actually added to the scene. 'I learned that day,' says Michel, 'not to be so single-minded and to embrace all opportunities.'

Canon EOS 5D Mark II + EF 16-35mm f2.8 lens; 1/85 sec at f5.6; ISO 400; Hugyfot housing.

The piranha-eater

HIGHLY COMMENDED

Marcelo Krause

BRAZIL

Most rivers in Brazil's Pantanal have zero visibility, and so photographing yacare caiman under water isn't easy, even though numbers have increased, following legal protection from hunting. In fact, photographing anything under water is difficult. When Marcelo entered the Vazante do Castelo river, it was the start of the dry season, when visibility is still reasonable. His intention was to photograph piranhas, but when he put out bait to attract them, several large yacare also arrived, probably attracted by all the movement and finding plenty of piranhas to eat. 'This huge one warned me off by opening its mouth,' says Marcelo. 'Then some of them started to bite my camera housing – time to get back in the boat.'

Nikon D2x + Tokina AT-X 107 AF 10-17mm f3.5-4.5 lens; 1/250 sec at f5.3; ISO 400; Aquatica D2 housing; Inon Z-240 strobe.

Manta-ray feast

HIGHLY COMMENDED

Michael AW

AUSTRALIA

From May and November, the lagoon on Hanifaru, a tiny islet in the Maldives, fills with plankton – a phenomenon thought to occur when lunar tides push against the Indian Ocean's monsoon current and suck plankton to the surface. Hundreds of manta rays go there to gorge, and Michael joined them. 'Nothing,' he says, 'could have prepared me for the exhilaration of being there. On occasions I was literally sucked into a spiral of huge mantas, bouncing off them, in and out, up and down. The excitement was too great to feel pain. Even with a fish-eye lens, it was impossible to capture the spectacle.'

Nikon D3 + 16mm f2.8 lens; 1/125 sec at f16; ISO 500; Seacam S45 housing; Ikelite S200 strobes.

It came from the gloom

HIGHLY COMMENDED

Patrik Bartuška

CZECH REPUBLIC

Patrik's sand-tiger location was a cave off South West Rocks, New South Wales, Australia. Sand tigers look fearsome but are quite placid, and Patrik's real anxiety was not to spook them. He flattened himself against the cave wall and tried to breathe shallowly so as not to produce too many bubbles. But though some sharks came so close that Patrik could almost touch them, he couldn't get the right shot. An hour later, frozen and low on air, he was about to surface when a 3-metre-long (10-foot) sand tiger appeared out of the gloom, followed by a school of eastern pomfred fish. It was the perfect moment, and Patrik got his shot.

Canon EOS 5D Mark II + 16-35mm f2.8 lens; 1/200 sec at f5.6; ISO 400; Seacam housing; Seacam Seaflash strobes.

Animal Portraits

This category – one of the most popular in the competition – invites portraits that capture the character or spirit of an animal in an original and memorable way.

Predatory steps

WINNER

Eirik Grønningsæter

NORWAY

This is the last view a seal might have. It's a viewpoint that Eirik set out to get when, from his boat, he spotted the polar bear resting close to shore on Kvalbeinøya, an island in the Arctic archipelago of Svalbard. Knowing that polar bears are insatiably curious, Eirik set up his camera on the snow, within sight of the bear, hoping that 'the ground view and wide angle lens would give a totally different kind of image'. Sure enough, the moment Eirik retreated to his boat, the bear made straight for the camera, checking it out from all angles, gently pushing it around. It even picked it up in its mouth. 'By not including the whole animal, I wanted to leave the end of the story untold,' says Eirik. The intimacy also conveys a powerful gentleness about the polar bear. When eventually it got bored and dropped the camera, there wasn't even a toothmark in the rubber.

Canon EOS 40D + 10-16mm f.2.8 lens; 1/250 sec at f13; ISO 640; remote control.

Dawn kill

SPECIALLY COMMENDED

Reto Puppetti

SWITZERLAND

At dawn in Kenya's Masai Mara, the roaring of lions alerted Reto and his guide to a hunt. By the time they located the pride, it had killed a wildebeest, and this male was fully occupied in feeding, giving Reto time to think about how he wanted to portray the scene. 'I prefer to show movement in an image, and I wanted to convey both the coldness of the morning and the melancholia of death,' he says. 'So I experimented with a long shutter speed, setting the white balance to tungsten, and I didn't freeze the action with a flash, which seemed more fitting to the wildness of such a magnificent predator.'

Canon EOS 5D Mark II + 400mm f5.6 lens; 1/5 sec at f5.6; ISO 640; Berlebach car-window mount.

Doug Brown

USA

The peregrine falcon had her work cut out. Her two youngsters had just started to fly, but they weren't yet skilled enough to catch their own prey, and so most of her time was spent hunting. Douglas had been photographing the family for more than a week and knew where the female's favourite perch was – a ledge near her nest on a steep cliff overlooking the Pacific in San Pedro, California. On this occasion, though, she chose to catch breath and scan for prey on the dead flower stem of a century plant. It was a precarious perch but provided a great photographic opportunity, with the peregrine framed by the curves of her strange perch and posed against a white backdrop of sky.

Canon EOS-1D Mark III + 500mm lens; 1/2000 sec at f5.6; ISO 640.

Oil beetle pose

HIGHLY COMMENDED

Juan Jesus Gonzalez Ahumada

SPAIN

This creature made a strange sight, clinging to a sprig of gorse on a cold spring morning in southern Spain. Close up, it reminded Juan of a beautiful alien. The black oil beetle is named after the toxic liquid it secretes if grabbed by a predator. As a larva, it lives in the burrow of a solitary bee, feeding on its pollen store and eggs, finally overwintering as a pupa and emerging as an adult in the spring. The female will lay her eggs in the vicinity of bee burrows, timed to hatch just after those of her host. Each louse-like beetle larva will then climb to the top of a flower and lie in wait to grab a lift on a bee and be carried back to its burrow, where it will grow, pupate and start the cycle again.

Canon EOS 40D + 100mm f2.8 lens; 1/4 sec at f8; ISO 100; Manfrotto 190 PRO tripod.

Giant beachcomber

HIGHLY COMMENDED

Thomas P. Peschak

SOUTH AFRICA/GERMANY

Aldabra giant tortoises normally graze on 'tortoise turf', a blend of herbs
and grasses that grows close to the ground in response to being cropped.
Often, though, the tortoises will wander onto the beaches to eat washed-up
seedpods. This female, who is probably at least 100 years old, regularly forages
along the beach in front of a research station on Aldabra in the Seychelles.
'Tortoises are known to have made sea crossings between islands,' says Tom,
'and so I was pleased to be able to use the ocean as a backdrop. I lay in her path
on the sand, using an extreme wide-angle lens. The moment I took the shot,
I had to roll out of her way to avoid her clambering right over me.'

Nikon D3 + 14-24mm lens; 1/200 sec at f22; ISO 200; Nikon SB800 flash.

The art of balance

HIGHLY COMMENDED

Roy Mangersnes

NORWAY

On the first day of heavy winter snow, Roy headed for Jæren, in southwest Norway, to photograph the snow-covered beaches. On the dunes, he found yellowhammers feeding on the remnants of wild rye poking out of the snow. 'I crept closer and waited until a few eventually came close enough,' he says. 'My aim was to create a simple composition with the grass, focusing on one bird but keeping a second one in the background, to add depth.' To Roy's amusement, his main subject had difficulty keeping its balance, 'stretching its wing out to the side for stability,' and adding an extra element to the design.

Nikon D3s + 70-200mm f2.8 lens; 1/2500 sec at f4; ISO 1250; Tc-14 converter.

Sunning griffon

HIGHLY COMMENDED

Oscar Díez

SPAIN

A griffon vulture holds out its huge wings to dry its feathers in the sun after heavy rain. What clinched the portrait for Oscar was not just the backlighting but also the pose as the magnificent vulture turned and looked straight in his direction. Oscar was, in fact, in a hide, at the feeding station near Ordesa and Monte Perdido National Park in the Spanish Pyrénées. Here sheep offal is put out as part of a conservation programme to help bearded vultures – a banquet that griffon vultures don't hesitate to join.

Canon EOS 40D + 500mm f4 lens; 1/500 sec at f7.1; ISO 250; tripod; hide.

One Earth Award

The pictures in this category can be graphic or symbolic but must be thought-provoking and memorable and encourage respect or concern for the natural world and our dependence on it.

Turtle in trouble

WINNER

Jordi Chias Pujol

SPAIN

It's an image that communicates in one emotive hit the damage being done to the world's oceans. Jordi came across this desperate scene when sailing between Barcelona and the Balearic Islands, hoping to photograph dolphins. 'I spotted the abandoned net drifting along the surface,' says Jordi. As he dived down to investigate, he could see the loggerhead turtle tangled up in the netting. 'The poor creature must have been trapped for some days, it was so badly knotted up.' Though it could just reach the surface to breathe by extending its neck, it was still sentenced to a long, cruel death. 'I felt as though it were looking at me for help as it tried to bite through the netting.' Jordi released it, allowing one individual a second chance. Given that all species of sea turtles are endangered, they need all the help they can get.

Nikon D300 + Tokina Fisheye 10-17mm f3.5-4.5 DX lens; 1/160 sec at f14; ISO 200; Inon strobes.

The last cut

RUNNER-UP

Daniel Beltrá

SPAIN

For the past eight years, Daniel has been documenting the destruction of the world's rainforests, focusing on the relationship between deforestation and global warming. One main reason for forest clearance in Indonesia is the consumption of palm oil, which is now used in half of all consumer goods, from cosmetics and prepacked food to biofuels. Here, in a new oil-palm plantation near Sungaihantu, Indonesia, on the island of Borneo, the skeleton of a rainforest tree is the last relic of the rainforest that once was. 'I want my photography to highlight how crucial it is to preserve these rich ecosystems – to inspire people to make changes that will help protect them,' says Daniel.

Canon EOS 5D Mark II + 100-400mm f4.5-5.6 lens; 1/1000 sec at f5.6; ISO 500.

Sacrifice

SPECIALLY COMMENDED

Steve Winter

USA

It took three days for this Asian elephant to die. It had been shot by villagers as it was rampaging through their crops after monsoon floods had forced it out of Kaziranga National Park in Assam, India. Though the shot itself didn't kill the elephant, the bullet had been soaked in acid, and the animal eventually died from septic poisoning. Here, a man prays in front of the body. 'Locals have a mixed relationship with elephants,' says Steve. 'They see them as dangerous and destructive and yet sacred, too,' icons of the Hindu elephant-headed deity Lord Ganesh.

Canon EOS 5D + 16-35mm f2.8 lens; 1/250 sec at f6.7; ISO 400.

Desecration in paradise

HIGHLY COMMENDED

Thomas Haider

AUSTRIA

Scientists have recently described the remote Raja Ampat islands of West Papua, Indonesia, as one of the world's richest marine ecosystems. But despite protection zones patrolled by boat and floatplane, migrant fishermen from Sulawesi, lured by high prices paid for shark fins, illegally shark-fish here. While on a research trip, Thomas spotted a boat fishing on the coral reef. As he drew closer, the fishermen threw their catch overboard. Taking his camera under water, Thomas faced this scene. 'A pristine reef offset by freshly mutilated sharks like exclamation marks. A desecration and a terrible waste.'

Nikon D3 + 14-24mm f2.8 lens; 1/125 sec at f14; ISO 200; Subal housing + Subal 10-inch dome port; Subtronic Nova flashlight.

Tears of blood

HIGHLY COMMENDED

Brian Skerry

USA

Each year more than 100 million sharks are killed worldwide, threatening the surival of most species. The slaughter is in part driven by the high price paid for shark fins on the Asian market. Brian went to Baja California, Mexico, specifically to document the killing. There is no restriction on shark-fishing in the Gulf of California, and using gillnets, fishermen will fish out an area and then move on. This female mako shark was pregnant with nearly full-term pups. 'I was concentrating on composing the frame to show the finning of this beautiful fish, with the fisherman sharpening his knife in the background,' says Brian. 'It was only afterwards that I noticed the poignant "tear of blood".'

Nikon D2x + 16mm lens; 1/125 sec at f11; ISO 100 .

103

Pot shot

HIGHLY COMMENDED

Sandesh Kadur

INDIA

In the hills of Meghalaya, northeast India, 'hunting is engrained in the culture,' says Sandesh. 'Everything is eaten.' Sandesh was photographing a pile of frogs that had been skinned and were drying in the sun when this little boy ran into his house and returned proudly holding a bird. 'He had shot the blue whistling thrush with a catapult that morning, and it was barely alive,' says Sandesh. Wildlife is becoming increasingly scarce in the area, not so much because of hunting but because of forest loss to logging, cultivation and development projects. The best hunting areas are now the few pockets of undisturbed natural vegetation, many of them supposedly protected areas.

Canon EOS 5D Mark II + 24-105mm f4 lens; 1/60 sec at f5; ISO 800.

The hidden plague

HIGHLY COMMENDED

Joel Sartore

USA

This is a crime scene in a remote corner of California, high in the Sixty Lakes Basin area of the Sierra Nevada: mountain yellow-legged frog corpses lie belly-up. The culprit is a chytrid fungus, which causes the infectious disease chytridiomycosis, implicated in the decline or rapid extinction of at least 200 species of frogs and other amphibians worldwide. The disease was first seen in dying frogs in the Sierra Nevada in 2004, since when it has reduced the population of mountain yellow-legged frogs from tens of thousands to under a hundred. The death of the frogs is emblematic of a global amphibian decline. It's believed that the fungus is being spread in part by the international trade in amphibians for display, food and laboratory use, its effects enhanced by global warming. Its impact on frogs has resulted in the biggest loss of vertebrate life due to disease ever recorded.

Nikon D3 + 14-24mm f2.8 lens; 1/160 sec at f22 (-0.3 e/v); ISO 400.

Gerald Durrell Award for Endangered Wildlife

The subjects featured here are species officially listed as critically endangered, endangered, vulnerable or at risk, and the purpose of the award is to highlight, through photographic excellence, the plight of wildlife under threat.

Tiger stalking

WINNER

Andy Rouse

UNITED KINGDOM

Tiger portraits are common enough (though tigers are most definitely not), but to photograph head-on the mesmerizing gaze of an intensely focused hunter is rare. This young tigress also gave Andy the chance to see a hunt from start to finish, on the very last drive of a recent trip to India. The young tigress stalked a herd of chital deer for a couple of hours through the long grass in Ranthambore National Park, while Andy stalked her. She followed the herd for more than a kilometre, constantly surveying for any sign of weakness or injury among the deer, before finally selecting her victim. Moments before she charged, Andy took his winning shot.

Nikon D3 + 200-400mm lens; 1/1000 sec at f4; ISO 500.

Survivor

HIGHLY COMMENDED

Neil Aldridge

SOUTH AFRICA

This is the lead female of a pack of African wild dogs living in South Africa's Venetia Limpopo Nature Reserve. Out of three litters, only one of her pups has survived. Predators got the rest, along with two of her mates. It's little surprise, then, that she is constantly alert. This, combined with the dense mopani vegetation, made photography a challenge. That Neil was able to get so close was by working alongside researchers studying the reserve's single pack and by lying on the tailgate of his Land Rover to get the low angle. The female's vigilance may help her protect her lone pup, but her endangered and persecuted species has declined to fewer than 5000 individuals scattered across a once vast range.

Canon EOS 1D Mark III + 400mm f2.8 lens + 1.4x converter; 1/800 sec at f4; ISO 200.

Night eyes

HIGHLY COMMENDED

Tim Laman

USA

Not once in 20 years of searching on the island of Borneo had Tim ever seen a Horsfield's (or western) tarsier. But he didn't give up his search for this small, rare and secretive primate. 'Tarsiers are totally nocturnal, so my goal was to capture the feel of night,' says Tim. Then, on a nocturnal sortie in the Danum Valley Conservation Area, Sabah, he finally found one. He raced back to the camp to get his tripod and strobe lights, and the tarsier cooperated, waiting and holding its pose. 'I kept my flash toned down and at an angle to illuminate the tarsier's special features: its toe pads for clinging to small trees, the sensitive, directional ears and those huge eyes for night vision.'

Canon EOS 5D + 70-200mm f2.8 lens; 1/125 sec at f11; ISO 200; Canon 580EX strobes.

Golden forest rhino

HIGHLY COMMENDED

Greg du Toit

SOUTH AFRICA

Greg's long-held ambition has been to photograph the critically endangered black rhino in a forest habitat. His trip to Lake Nakuru, Kenya, had an inauspicious start when he dropped his lens, losing the zoom and VR (vibration-reduction) functions. And his subject – renowned for being shy – completely eluded him. On the last day, at first light, he went for the last time into the ancient fever-tree forest. It was then that he finally spotted what he'd been waiting for, browsing on a fallen tree. 'I was shaking with excitement,' he confesses, 'which posed a problem without VR, and the forest was so dark that my shutter speed sank.' His old beanbag came to the rescue as a prop for his lens, enabling him finally to capture the magnificent animal in the golden light of dawn.

Nikon D300 + 80-400mm lens; 1/60 sec at f5.6; ISO 400; beanbag.

Fishing frenzy

HIGHLY COMMENDED

Tomasz Raczyński

POLAND

Tomasz is an observer on commercial pelagic trawlers in the South Pacific, which gives him the perfect opportunity for seabird photography – the equivalent, he says, of being on a huge birdtable at sea. Fish falling from the nets as they are pulled up are an irresistible lure. Here, a black-browed albatross has just surfaced after diving for the discarded horse mackerel and is being set upon by a rabble of other birds. By comparison to the albatross-friendly trawlers, longline-fishing ships are death traps – the cause of the decline of 18 out of the 22 species of albatross. Their hooked lines, set to catch fish such as tuna and toothfish, can be miles long and kill an estimated 100,000 albatrosses annually.

Nikon D3 + 80-200mm f2.8D lens; 1/1250 sec at f8; ISO 1000.

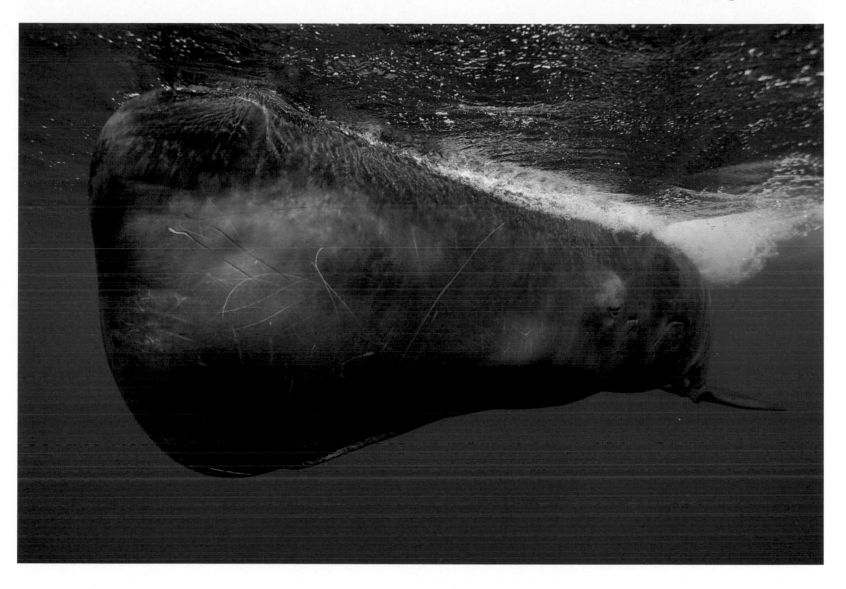

Giant encounter

HIGHLY COMMENDED

Tony Wu

USA

Scar, a ten-year-old sperm whale, loves playing with people as much as he does with the other sperm whales in his group. Injured as a calf off Dominica, where he was born, possibly by a pod of pilot whales, he has since bonded with people and invites contact. Scar came right up to Tony when he was snorkelling, resulting in an unusual perspective of the world's largest predator. His massive head is a third of his body length, and he may well grow to be up to 18 metres (59 feet) long. Says Tony, 'It's a bit unnerving when you're in the water and a nearly full-grown whale charges at you at high speed – and you're not 100 per cent sure it's Scar.'

Canon 5D Mark II + 17-40mm f4 lens; 1/200 sec at f7.1, ISO 200, Zillion housing; Pro One optical dome port.

Pelican pack

HIGHLY COMMENDED

Jari Peltomäki

FINLAND

By February, when Jari arrived at Lake Kerkini, many of the Dalmatian pelicans were already in their breeding plumage, the males displaying their orange-red throat pouches. Numbers have declined dramatically, but in winter, hundreds congregate on the lake in northern Greece. 'Local fishermen have a special relationship with them and feed them scraps,' says Jari. 'The pelicans follow the men around, and so I tagged along, too.' He used a floating hide to get the water-level angle he needed. His aim was to light them with the rising sun against a backdrop of the snow-covered mountains – which he did, to perfection, as the birds reached skyward for scraps thrown from a nearby boat.

Canon EOS-1D Mark III + 70-200mm f2.8 lens; 1/2000 sec at f10; ISO 800; angled viewfinder + Finnature ground pod.

Wildlife Photojournalist of the Year Award

This award is given to a sequence of six pictures that tells a memorable story, whether about behaviour or an environmental issue. The sequence has to work without the aid of words and is judged on picture quality as well as the power of the story itself.

Mark Leong

USA

'IT'S JUST AN ANIMAL'

Medicine, cosmetics, food, luxury goods, fashion, entertainment, aquariums, interior design, pets … the international markets for wildlife and wildlife products are insatiable, and the illegal trade in rare and endangered species is thriving. Mark's reportage captures the ignorance, apathy, corruption and cruelty that sustain this multi-billion-dollar industry.

The skin trade

Every day, workers in Rantau Prapat, Sumatra, slaughter and skin hundreds of reptiles brought to them by trappers. 'There were masses of tied-up sacks full of live pythons and monitor lizards,' says Mark. 'The men kill or at least stun each animal with a blow to the head. Then they fill the snake with water and air to make it easier to slit open, gut and skin.' The dried skins are sold to the international leather-goods industry, to be made into luxury and fashion items such as wallets, belts and boots. The gall bladders go to Chinese traditional medicine dealers. 'I wanted to convey both the volume of the processing as well as the hellish element of this assembly line, to get across the message that this is an industrial-scale wild-animal trade.'

Nikon D2x + Sigma 14mm f2.8 aspherical lens; 1/60 sec at f4; ISO 320.

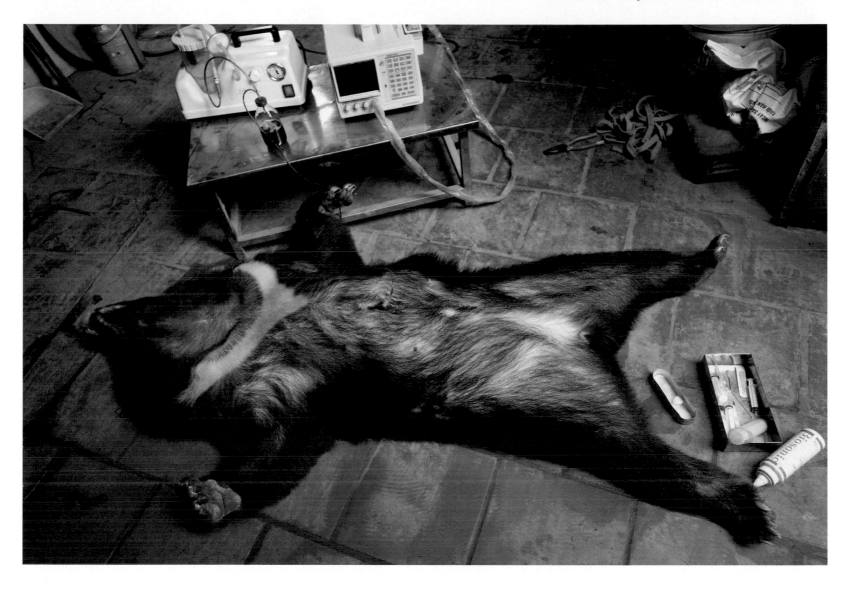

Supplying demand

A remedy for impotence, liver disease, hangovers and more, bear bile is highly valued in Chinese medicine. Near Hanoi, Vietnam, a sedated Asiatic black bear is illegally pumped for bile, one of thousands of bears kept for this purpose throughout Asia. First, the bear is drugged. When it is unconscious or just partly conscious, the extractors use an ultrasound machine to find the gall bladder. They insert a long needle, attach a tube and pump 100–150cc of bile into a bottle. The whole process takes up to 20 minutes. 'The bear looked almost human, so vulnerable,' says Mark. 'The market for bile is strong, and with little government enforcement of the law, this practice is pretty widespread across Vietnam. Bile is often openly advertised by the side of the road.'

Nikon D700 + 17-35mm f2.8 lens; 1/60 sec at f4.5; ISO 1250.

Market goods

Wild birds (here a spotted wood owl and a wreathed hornbill), primates such as these long-tailed macaques, leopard cats, snakes and other animals, many of them banned from trade, are sold openly in the middle of urban Jakarta, West Java, Indonesia. For the traders, it's day-to-day business. Unlike Jakarta's bigger, more central wildlife trade centre, the Pramuka Market, this one is much less covert and much easier to photograph. No one challenges the pet-sellers, and the authorities are nowhere to be seen. The market is popular and gets very busy after work or school and at the weekend. 'For many people, it's just another kind of recreation, somewhere to go, something to do, like browsing for shoes or clothes,' says Mark. 'The hardest challenge conservation bodies face is the widespread "it's only an animal" mindset that so many people have.'

Nikon D700 + 17-35mm f2.8 lens; 1/80 sec at f5.6; ISO 200.

The making of a pet

At the Jatinegara Bird and Pet Market in Jakarta, West Java, wild-caught animals such as young long-tailed macaques are sold illegally alongside rabbits, goldfish and other legally traded, captive-bred pets. To stop them biting their owners, macaques have their sharp teeth blunted. Mark describes what happened when one pet-trader summoned him over to photograph how he did it. 'He put his hand in the cage and pulled out one of the young macaques. It had seen what had happened to others and was squeaking with fear. Using pliers and a whetstone, the man trimmed and filed the monkey's teeth. For many of these pictures, I shot with the focused remoteness that photography allows and sometimes requires. But for this shot I was right there with the macaque, imagining all that snapping and grinding being done to my teeth. It was excruciatingly painful to watch.'

Nikon D700 + 17-35mm f2.8 lens; 1/80 sec at f5.6; ISO 800; SB800 flash.

Tiger-farm show

Every day, animals at the Xiongsen Bear and Tiger Park of Guilin, Guangxi, China, perform in circus-style shows – an easily accessible tourist attraction near the city's airport. The park, which owns more than 400 bears and 1300 tigers, claims to be working for conservation by keeping them safe in captivity. But it has also lobbied for lifting regulations on the tiger-trade ban, especially when it comes to tiger-bone wine (the park has an attached distillery). DNA tests on food from the park restaurant subsequently revealed that it was illegally serving tiger meat. 'There has been speculation that some so-called zoos or parks may be stockpiling animals in anticipation of a change in the law, which would allow them to utilize captive-bred tigers legally,' says Mark.

Nikon D2x + 17-35mm f2.8 lens; 1/50 sec at f3.2; ISO 400.

The orphans

Orangutans confiscated from circuses, sideshows and private owners in Kalimantan, Indonesia, are taken in by the Borneo Orangutan Survival Foundation. The orphans go to 'forest school' – the rainforest – where they can practise skills such as climbing and learn which plants are edible. Mark included the shot to show that not all interaction with Asian animals is consumptive. 'The hardest part of this shoot,' says Mark, 'was resisting the urge to play with the little ones, because they are so social, curious and adorable.' It was important that he didn't, though, because there's one more crucial skill these orphans must learn if they are ever to be released back into the forest: to be wary of humans. But, of course, they can only ever be released if there is forest rather than oil-palm plantations for them to live in.

Nikon D2x + 17-35mm f2.8 lens; 1/50 sec at f7.1; ISO 100.

Wildlife Photojournalist
of the Year Award

RUNNER-UP

Brian Skerry

USA

THE MOST SHOCKING STORY OF ALL

The oceans are in deep trouble. We treat them as if their resources
are infinite and their capacity to deal with whatever we throw into
them is unlimited. But though millions of people depend on fish for
protein, fish populations worldwide are crashing. This photo-story
was shot to help raise awareness of the issues surrounding industrial
fisheries – in particular, the methods used to gather fish, and the
rapidly dwindling stocks.

Last of the tuna

To supply the world's sushi markets, bluefin tuna are fished from the Mediterranean at four times the sustainable rate. They are then fattened up in 69 ranches (here, fresh from the wild in a pen off the San Pedro del Pinatar, Spain) that have sprung up in the Mediterranean over the past decade. 'Bluefin tuna continue to grow throughout their long lives, crisscross entire oceans annually and are capable of swimming nearly from the equator to the poles,' says Brian, who describes them as 'one of the most incredible animals that has ever lived.' But their populations are crashing through overfishing, legal and illegal, and despite calls for a temporary ban on global trade to let numbers build up, tuna continue to be hunted – probably to extinction in the very near future.

Nikon D2X + 14mm lens; 1/60 sec at f9; ISO 250; Subal housing; Hartenberger strobes.

The commodity market

Every day, bluefin tuna are brought from all over the world to the Tsukiji Fish Market in Tokyo. Laid out across the floor, they are auctioned off before sunrise, destined for Japanese raw-fish sushi and sashimi. In 2009, a single bluefin tuna sold for nearly $180,000. Brian wandered through warehouses containing the finned, gutted and skinless bodies. 'It was disturbing', he says, 'to see such magnificent and increasingly scarce animals transformed into commodities. The ocean is not a grocery store for our convenience, and we can't continue to fish at this scale without serious consequences.' But for the commodity dealers, continuing to overfish tuna makes economic sense: the fewer tuna there are in the world, the higher the price they fetch.

Nikon D3 + 14-24mm lens; 1/30 sec at f5.6; ISO 1600.

Scraping the bottom

This is how shrimps (prawns) are caught off La Paz in the Sea of Cortez, Mexico. Whether a trawl net is small, like this one, or large, the design is similar worldwide: two steel doors help keep open the maw of the net as a boat drags it along. Such a design is hugely effective, catching shrimps but also everything else in its path. As it drags along the bottom, it also destroys whole communities, including the corals and sponges that provide habitat for so many other animals and which may take years to grow back.

Nikon D2X + 16mm lens; 1/160 sec at f11; ISO 320; Subal housing; Sea & Sea YS90 strobes.

The true cost of shrimps

An hour's worth of towing his net off La Paz, Sea of Cortez, Mexico, and this fisherman had a handful – literally – of valuable shrimps (prawns) to show for it. The 5 kilograms (11 pounds) or so of other species caught unintentionally will be dumped back into the sea. This is legal but completely unregulated. Driven by the growing international appetite for shrimps, fishermen will do what it takes to make a living, whatever the cost to the other animals in the sea. And consumers in the west, unaware of, or choosing to ignore, what's happening out of view, will continue to demand shrimps on the menu.

Nikon D2X + 12-24mm lens; 1/60 sec at f9; ISO 200.

Waste products

Uncannily beautiful, this scene shows a cascade of dead fish, including guitarfish and rays, tossed from a Mexican shrimp boat. It's the incidental, unwanted bycatch from one small net on one short trawl – tiny compared to the devastation caused by industrial-scale nets several kilometres long. In fact, worldwide, millions of tonnes of marine animals are caught unintentionally each year and thrown back into the sea as trash.

Nikon D2X + 16mm lens; 1/125 sec at f9; ISO 100; Subal housing; Sea & Sea YS90 strobes.

The sacrifice

Entangled in a gillnet, this bigeye thresher shark is just one of an estimated 100 million sharks killed each year, many unintentionally, in the thousands of kilometres of gillnets strung out in the world's oceans. Sharks play a vital role in maintaining healthy ecosystems, and so their removal has long-lasting repercussions on fish stocks. Brian struggled for months to think of a way to represent the slaughter of sharks that would move people rather than just shock them. When he saw this scene, he knew he had found the symbolic image he needed. He was on a dive documenting the bycatch of gillnets in the Sea of Cortez. 'The shark had only just died, and it seemed to be looking directly at me, its pectoral fins outstretched as if in crucifixion.' Gillnets and longlines set by commercial fishing operations have wiped out more than 90 per cent of the predatory fish species in the Sea of Cortez.

Nikon D2X + 16mm lens; 1/60 sec at f8; ISO 100; Subal housing; Sea & Sea YS90 strobes.

Wildlife Photojournalist of the Year Award

SPECIALLY COMMENDED

Kai Fagerström

FINLAND

THE HOUSE IN THE WOODS

The house appears deserted. The roof has holes and the walls are crumbling. Draughts hiss through the windows. Floorboards crack, and doors creak. But if you hang around until dusk, if you listen and watch and are patient, you may glimpse inhabitants; because when people move out, nature moves in.

Sunset

The sun's last rays bounce off the old windowpanes, as though a fire roars within. This house near Salo, Finland, is probably at least 200 years old, but the last people moved on more than 30 years ago. As darkness falls, though, the house comes alive.

Nikon D3 + 50mm f1.2 lens; 8 sec at f2.8; ISO 800.

Yellow-necked mouse wakes

Toys, pots, a lampshade, old-fashioned shoes ... the last people to move out left many of their belongings behind. 'It's as though time stood still,' says Kai. 'Who were they? What was their daily life like?' The routine of the yellow-necked mouse, though, was easy to work out. 'I scattered nuts among a group of dusty old wine bottles to attract it. But many days passed before conditions were right, and the setting sun threw shadows on the peeling, textured wallpaper. I then just had to wait until the mouse turned up.'

Nikon D3 + 70-200mm f2.8 lens; 1/1250 sec at f4; ISO 6400.

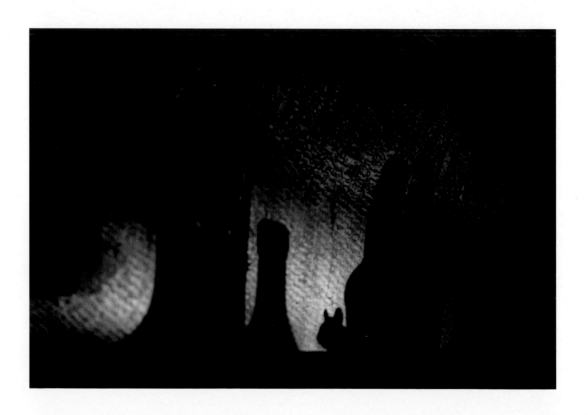

Raccoon dog drops by

A litter of ten raccoon dog puppies had been born in the woods that year. One pup soon began to explore the garden, foraging under the berry bushes and apple trees. A creature of habit, it dropped by at the same time every night. Then it began visiting the house. 'At night, the light can be beautiful, and on this particular evening, it was perfect.' Here the raccoon dog pauses by the half-open door, sniffing the air. A moment later, he melted back into the night. In autumn, the raccoon dog stopped coming. Maybe, like most raccoon dog pups, it didn't survive. Or maybe it settled into a den in the woods and lives close by.

Nikon D3 + 17-35mm f2.8 lens; 1/30 sec at f2.8; ISO 200.

Pygmy owl comes home

This pygmy owl was more than a passing visitor. It seemed to know the house well and may even have lived there at one time. It would certainly have known that there were mice to catch in the house. 'It wasn't too shy, so photographing it was quite easy,' says Kai, though the lighting was difficult against the snow outside. But the owl wasn't happy that Kai was in the house. 'It seemed to stamp its foot and say, "Go away, this is my place ..." So I went.'

Nikon F5 + 70-200mm f2.8 lens; 1/125 sec at f2.8; Agfa RSX 100.

Red squirrel keeps a lookout

Red squirrels often build their dreys inside abandoned houses, and so Kai
was not in the least surprised to discover one inside the house. The house
gave shelter in winter and safety from hungry birds of prey. Kai tempted the
squirrel onto the window ledge with nuts so he could photograph it against
the window and the ancient, shredded curtains. 'I love the fact that it is looking
out of the window,' he says, 'as though expecting guests to arrive any minute.'

Nikon D3 + 85mm f1.4 lens; 1/30 sec at f4; ISO 1000.

The badgers at home

These cubs were born in a sett under the floorboards, and the fireplace was
their entrance to the house. The cubs loved exploring and quickly learnt to
climb the stairs to the bedrooms. Taking the picture through the window,
Kai wanted to give an impression of the badger family going about its daily
business. Badgers are his favourite forest animal, but in Finland they are very
wary of humans. They have reason to be – around 10,000 are killed each year
by hunters, partly out of a misconception that they harm wild-bird populations
(the bulk of their diet is, in fact, worms and other invertebrates; only
occasionally do they eat chicks). 'Badgers hardly feature in Finnish folklore,'
says Kai, 'and people don't realize what fascinating characters they really are.'

Eric Hosking Award

The aim of this award is to encourage talented young photographers aged 18 to 26. It is given for a portfolio of six images representing the photographer's best work.

The award goes to Bence Máté from Hungary. Bence was the Young Wildlife Photographer of the Year in 2003 and went on to win the Eric Hosking Award, first when he was just 19 and then again two years later. He built his first tailor-made viewing hide at the age of 14 and is now an expert creator of hides, which he uses in conjunction with the photography tours he now runs. For much of the past year, Bence has been living in Costa Rica and Brazil, making use of his own brand of bird-photography hides.

Leg-work

When photographing birds from his waterside hide in Hungary's Kiskunsági National Park, Bence would sleep in the hide. It was the only way to photograph the birds at dawn (entering the hide at that time would have disturbed them). Bence rigged up a special setup to get a water-level view of his subjects. 'The camera was in an aquarium 3 metres (11 feet) away, linked to my laptop,' says Bence. 'So whenever I took a picture, I could immediately see it on the screen.' To get around the problem of the birds smearing the aquarium with muck, he fixed a spool of transparent printer's film to the front, so he could, by remote control, roll around a clean piece. 'This technique, plus my fisheye lens, gave me a new perspective.' This shot is his favourite – a grey heron that had perched on the hide suddenly swooped down on a great white egret standing on the aquarium. The legs are the heron's, the wings the egret's.

Nikon D300 + Tamron 10-17mm f3.5-4.5 lens; 1/250 sec at f16; ISO 200; 3pc SB-800 flash; remote tripod head; hide.

A marvel of ants

When Bence first tried to photograph leaf-cutter ants in action, he thought it was going to be easy. It wasn't, but relishing the challenge, he found out as much as he could about their complex society and spent hours watching and following them in the Costa Rican rainforest. 'They proved to be wonderful subjects,' says Bence, who discovered that they were most active at night. He would follow a column as it fanned out into the forest. Each line terminated at a tree, shrub or bush. 'The variation in the size of the pieces they cut was fascinating – sometimes small ants seemed to carry huge bits, bigger ones just small pieces.' Of his winning shot, he says, 'I love the contrast between the simplicity of the shot itself and the complexity of the behaviour.' Lying on the ground to take the shot, he also discovered the behaviour of chiggers (skin-digesting mite larvae), which covered him in bites. (See also page 14.)

Nikon D700 + 105mm f2.8 lens; 1/200 sec at f10; ISO 640; SB-800 flash.

Caiman's little mouthful

It's not often that wildlife photographers simply come across a subject.
This, though, was just about as spontaneous as a shot can be. Bence had spent
a long, hard day building a hide. As he headed back to his lodge in Brazil's
Pantanal, he encountered a 3-metre-long (11-foot) caiman ambling across the
lawn. Dangling from its jaws were the remains of a young armadillo. In the dry
season, caimans are forced to venture farther afield to hunt, but it's rare to see
one with prey. 'I raced to get my telephoto lens,' says Bence. 'By the time I got
back, the caiman was nearly at the river, so I dropped to my knees and started
shooting. I had no strategy, no plan, no hide. I was so lucky to get the shot.'

Nikon D700 + 300mm f2.8 lens; 1/2500 sec at f5; ISO 800.

Attention time

The newly fledged burrowing owl chicks (here, each balancing on one leg, with the female attending to some necessary grooming) still couldn't fly. They had emerged from their den only three days before. But they were impossible to photograph for much of the day. 'In the sweltering heat, they would tuck themselves into the shade of my hide.' But as soon as the temperature cooled, they would flutter up to the top of the spoil-heap created when their parents had first excavated the nest hole. So every day for a week, Bence would crawl into his hide at about 6pm to photograph them in the short window of opportunity before the sun set over the Pantanal.

Nikon D700 + 300mm f2.8 lens; 1/320 sec at f2.8; ISO 1600; Gitzo tripod; hide.

Fire on the Pantanal

Walking back one evening from his hide to the farm where he was staying, Bence first smelt the fire. Turning off the trail, he came to 'the awe-inspiring sight' of a curtain of fire stretching across the Pantanal. It may have been started naturally or by cattle farmers clearing the land to stimulate grass growth. 'The tallest flames must have been nearly 5 metres [16 feet] high,' says Bence. 'With such intense firelight, it was a challenge to work out how to photograph the scene. I used a long-exposure and stretched out my arm to cover the flames with my hands to expose the stars. Then, for the last second or so, I took away my hands to expose the flames.' With the crackling noise and the intensity of the heat, it was a memorable event. 'At times, the smoke was terrible. But at least it kept the mosquitoes away.'

Nikon D700 + 20mm f2.8 lens; 20 sec at f2.8; ISO 1000; Gitzo tripod.

King of the vultures

After two months of labour, Bence's hide was finally excavated and the king vulture banquet ready. 'I'd seen nothing but black vultures for weeks,' he says. 'So I'd been to the nearest town, 40 kilometres [25 miles] away from where I was staying in northern Costa Rica, to see if I could scrounge a carcass that might attract a king.' A sympathetic butcher gave him three cow heads. 'I knew that king vultures can smell fresh meat from several kilometres away, but it was a great surprise to me when they turned up almost straight away.' With a powerful, sharp beak, complete with a meat hook, and a rasping, flesh-stripping tongue, a king vulture (right) is itself a bit like butcher. It is often the first vulture to rip open a tough carcass, and this allows other vultures such as the black vulture (left) access to the softer meat inside.

Nikon D300 + Sigma 300-800mm f5.6 lens; 1/4000 sec at f8; ISO 800; Gitzo tripod.

The Veolia Environnement Young Wildlife Photographer of the Year Award

The title Veolia Environnement Young Wildlife Photographer of the Year 2010 and a cash prize goes to Fergus Gill – the young photographer whose image has been judged to be the most memorable of all the pictures by photographers aged 17 or under.

Fergus Gill

UNITED KINGDOM

Living in rural Scotland, Fergus has been interested in nature since he was very young. He started taking photographs at the age of nine, when his father encouraged him to carry a camera to record what he saw. At 14, he won first prize in his age category in this competition, which gave him the confidence to pursue nature photography as a serious interest. Then last year, he was the winner of this major award. He concentrates in particular on the wildlife near his home. Indeed, the vast majority of his photography occurs in his back garden.

The frozen moment

WINNER (15–17 YEARS)

On Boxing Day 2009, it was so cold in Scotland (-17°C /1°F) that the birds were desperate for food. A rowan tree at the bottom of Fergus's garden in Perthshire became a magnet for thrushes – five of the six British species – song thrushes, mistle thrushes, blackbirds, redwings and a flock of about 15 fieldfares, all frantically picking the berries. Fergus wanted to capture the freezing feel of the day while showing the character of fieldfares in action, some of which were hovering to pluck berries. His biggest challenge (other than the cold itself) was to isolate a fieldfare against a clear background, and the only way to get the angle was to stand on his frozen pond. Risking a high ISO setting as well as the ice, he caught both the moment and the delicacy of colour he was after.

Light projection

RUNNER-UP (15–17 YEARS)

Michal Budzyński

POLAND

Michal is fascinated by the way simple subjects such as light, snow and trees can create myriad forms, patterns and scenes, and he's always experimenting with unusual compositions. He went to the Beskidy Mountains in southern Poland to photograph the winter landscapes there. Shivering after standing for several hours at dawn in temperatures below -15°C (5°F), his attention was caught by a sliver of golden sunlight crossing the snow. 'I focused on the backlit silhouette of the tree,' he says. 'The empty space at the bottom emphasizes the simplicity. It reminds me of a stained-glass window.'

Nikon D80 + 80-200mm f2.8 lens; 1/30 sec at f11; ISO 100; Manfrotto tripod.

Deer at dusk

SPECIALLY COMMENDED (15–17 YEARS)

Jack Chapman

UNITED KINGDOM

Jack was learning to drive, and while on holiday in the Scottish Highlands, he took advantage of being allowed to practise using the family car and headed up to Loch Garry to do some landscape photography. As the light began to fade at the end of the day, he noticed that red deer were gathering on the loch shore. Jack changed to a short lens, knowing that the lack of light meant there was no point in trying to take a portrait. 'Even then I struggled with shutter speeds and focusing,' he says. He was still trying out different compositions when it started to rain. But it was the resulting clouds banked up on the mountains opposite that helped create the moody atmosphere he was after.

Canon EOS 40D + 18-55mm lens; 0.5 sec at f5.6; ISO 640; tripod.

Chick delight

HIGHLY COMMENDED

Johan Gehrisch

SWEDEN

Johan was at Látrabjarg, Iceland – Europe's most westerly point – when he discovered a colony of hundreds of Arctic terns nesting in a field. This nest, nothing more than a scrape in the ground, was close enough to the road for the car to be used as a hide (had he got out, he would not only have disturbed the birds but would have been dive-bombed by the angry adults). The chicks were gaping hard. They would need all the food they could get before heading to Antarctica. Artic terns undertake the longest annual migration in the animal kingdom, spending the southern summer in Antarctica and returning to the Arctic in the northern spring to breed.

Canon EOS 50D + 200mm f2.8 lens + 2x converter; 1/500 sec at f8; ISO 640.

Eye for a bird

HIGHLY COMMENDED

Fergus Gill

UNITED KINGDOM

Fergus's favourite place to be is in the Scottish Cairngorms in winter.
'I have such respect for the animals that survive here, especially ptarmigan.'
Alert to danger but relying on its camouflage to keep safe, this ptarmigan
watched Fergus's every move as, having spotted the bird's head, Fergus crept
up a mountain slope, climbed over a ridge, traversed down it and then crawled
through a rock field to get to a vantage point where he could start taking
pictures. The ptarmigan stayed put for half an hour and then suddenly turned
and faced the afternoon sun. 'I love the simplicity,' says Fergus, 'the subtle light
caught in his eye and the hint of red wattle above.'

Nikon D300 + 500mm f4 lens; 1/400 sec at f5.6; ISO 400.

First snow

HIGHLY COMMENDED

Ilari Miikka Kalevi Tuupanen

FINLAND

The alarm clock went off at dawn, and Ilari and his dad headed out into the dark, climbed into their motorboat and crossed Lake Ruunaa in North Karelia, Finland, to a swamp they'd been exploring. It was still quite dark when they got there, too dark to take any photographs. 'Moments later, we saw a bear,' says Ilari. 'That was a great experience, even though I didn't get a picture.' As the sun rose, Ilari was able to start taking photographs. But it wasn't until they were returning to the boat that it started to snow. 'I took the last few photos from the beach,' says Ilari. 'With snow everywhere, the landscape looked so beautiful. Winter was coming.'

Canon EOS 40D + Tamron 200-400mm f5.6 lens; 1/60 sec at f8; ISO 320.

Crane perfection

WINNER (11–14 YEARS)

Martin Gregus Jr.

CANADA/SLOVAKIA

This sandhill crane was totally absorbed preening and cleaning its feathers – so busy that Martin was able to spend more than an hour lying on the ground nearby photographing it. Martin was at the George C. Reifel Migratory Bird Sanctuary near Vancouver, Canada, where there are a few pairs of resident sandhill cranes. When they groom, the cranes sometimes emerge from the marsh onto the paths. Knowing this, Martin had spent the afternoon waiting for such a chance. 'I like the way that the very low angle makes the bird appear grandiose and his colour and structure contrast with the blue sky,' says Martin.

Nikon D70 + 18-35mm f3.5-4.5 lens at 35mm; 1/1600 sec at f4.5; ISO 220.

Swan loch

RUNNER-UP (11–14 YEARS)

Sam Cairns

UNITED KINGDOM

'Winter is my favourite season,' says Sam, 'for photography and also for the sheer beauty of it.' A prolonged period of sub-zero temperatures, snow and clear skies generated plenty of photographic opportunities in the Cairngorms National Park, near where he lives in Scotland. An unusually striking sunset drew him to this loch and its mute swans, 'elegantly floating in the ice-free water'. Setting up on the bridge across the loch, Sam began to take photos as the sunset colours intensified and then faded. 'Nearly 250 frames later, I had the image I wanted,' says Sam. 'To me, it proves that you don't need to go somewhere exotic to photograph something sensational.'

Canon EOS-1Ds Mark II + 24-105mm lens; 1/20 sec at f4; ISO 500; Gitzo tripod.

Roe in snow

HIGHLY COMMENDED

Arthur-Coriolan Wilmotte

FRANCE

A winter scene like this in southwest France is unusual, and when it snowed for the second time last winter, Arthur-Coriolan set out very early one morning to take photos. But after an hour and a half, he had found only the tracks of a hare and a deer. Then, as it started to get light, a pair of roe deer appeared in the distance. His lens wasn't able to zoom in on the animals, and so he decided to compose an image that made the most of the surroundings and to experiment with the diagonal lines of the ploughed field. 'I'm glad I couldn't take a close-up portrait of the deer,' he says. 'I prefer the minimalist atmosphere, which reflects that bitterly cold morning.'

Nikon D60 + 70-300mm lens; 1/100 sec at f11; ISO 800; tripod

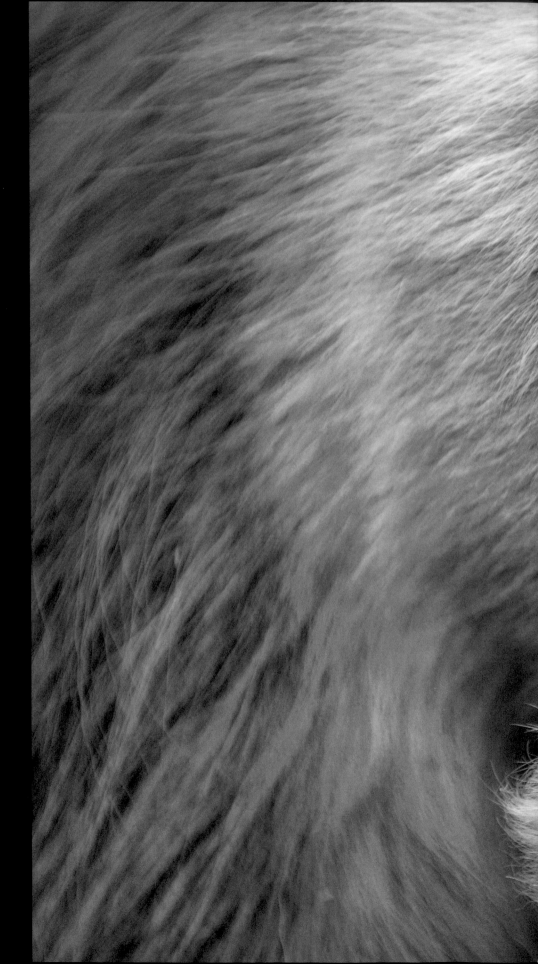

Golden monkey

WINNER (10 YEARS AND UNDER)

Haijun Pei

CHINA

Haijun and his parents went to China's Qingling
Mountains, Shaanxi, in winter, to search for the
endangered golden snub-nosed monkey. They
found a troop of monkeys drinking from a river,
climbing trees, jumping and basking in the sun.
'They were so beautiful, with their long golden
hair and blue faces,' Haijun says. 'The young ones
played together like mischievous children.'
The monkeys' main food is lichen, but they also
eat fruits, seeds, leaves and bark, and Haijun
noticed white marks on tree trunks made by
the monkeys gnawing the bark. The camera that
Haijun used was so heavy that he had to balance
it on his knee to use it. 'I love the golden
snub-nosed monkey,' he says.

**Nikon D3 + 70-200mm f2.8 lens at 200mm; 1/500 sec at
f3.5; ISO 800.**

Golden moment

HIGHLY COMMENDED

Malte Parmo

DENMARK

'The bearded tit,' says Malte, 'is one of my favourite birds.' So he couldn't believe his luck when, while on a photography trip with his father to the Vest Amager wetland, close to Copenhagen, Denmark, they heard its characteristic *psching* call. Hoping for a chance of photographing it, they set off into the reeds. He went one way, his father another. Then something amazing happened: a flock of bearded tits landed right in front of Malte and started to feed, lit by the low December sun and dappled by the shadows of the reeds. This male wasn't at all bothered by his presence, and so Malte was able to just stand and take photographs. 'I couldn't believe my luck,' he says.

Canon EOS 450D + 70-200mm f4 lens + 1.4x converter; 1/500 sec at f6.3; ISO 400.

Super-toad

RUNNER-UP (10 YEARS AND UNDER)

Will Jenkins

UNITED KINGDOM

One morning, when a big common toad lumbered onto the patio of his house in London, Will abandoned breakfast, gathered up the sofa cushions, set up the two family cameras and settled down on his tummy to watch. 'Toads are brilliantly warty and ugly,' he says. 'I was hoping to photograph it catching a fly.' He watched for an hour. Then, suddenly, the cat-flap rattled. 'The cat was too fat to get through, but the toad seemed scared by the noise. So I made a ramp with a plank so it could get back to the grass.' The toad took a couple of steps and then leapt away. 'I caught my toad in the air, and I love that. Despite being a little guy, his legs shot him a long way. He was so fast, flying like a superhero.'

Canon 20D + 18-55mm lens; 1/50 sec at f5.6; ISO 100.

Bringing back breakfast

HIGHLY COMMENDED

Lucas Marsalle

FRANCE

For several years, a pair of kestrels has nested in a hole in the wall under a mountain road near where Lucas lives in Aure, in the French Pyrénées. Last year, his father built a hide so they could watch the birds. It overlooked the kestrels' favourite perch, where they would land before flying into the nest hole. Lucas and his father would get up when it was still dark so that they could be in the hide by dawn without the kestrels realizing they were there. Here the male kestrel, clutching breakfast for its newly hatched chicks, pauses for a few moments in the first rays of sun, giving Lucas the perfect pose for a photograph.

Nikon D300 + 500mm lens; 1/1000 sec at f5.6; ISO 400; tripod; hide.

Sitting out the storm

HIGHLY COMMENDED

Russell T. Laman

USA

Russell took a horse-drawn sleigh-ride through the National Elk Refuge at Jackson Hole, Wyoming, USA, hoping to photograph the elk – one of the largest species of deer in the world. 'We specifically chose a snowy day,' says Russell, 'because I thought I could get more interesting pictures of them in harsh winter conditions.' The visibility was poor but the stags' profiles were clear as they sat out the storm. 'I especially liked this picture,' says Russell, 'because of the strong sense of atmosphere and the way the elk in the background almost mirrors the one in front.'

Canon EOS 20D + 100-300mm lens; 1/500 sec at f19; ISO 400.

Index of photographers

108
Neil Aldridge (South Africa)
neil@conservationphotojournalism.com
www.neilaldridge.wordpress.com

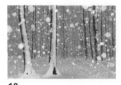

18
Sandra Bartocha (Germany)
info@bartocha-photography.com
www.bartocha-photography.com

93
Doug Brown (USA)
birdphotog@me.com
http://web.me.com/birdphotog

148
Sam Cairns (UK)
samcairns32@hotmail.com
www.samcairns.com

45
Matt Cole (UK)
matt.cole2@gmail.com
www.mattcolephotography.co.uk

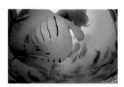

88
Michael AW (Australia)
one@michaelaw.com
www.michaelaw.com

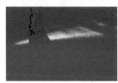

63
Sandra Bartocha (Germany)/
Wild Wonders of Europe
info@bartocha-photography.com
www.bartocha-photography.com
www.wild-wonders.com

140
Michal Budzyński (Poland)
mail@michalbudzynski.com
www.michalbudzynski.com

29
Jordan Calame (USA)
manitobatc@gmail.com

68
Ben Cranke (South Africa/UK)
ben@bencranke.com
bencranke.com
Agent
www.gettyimages.co.uk

28
Adrian Bailey (South Africa)
info@baileyphotos.com
www.baileyphotos.com
Agent
www.auroraphotos.com

89
Patrik Bartuška (Czech Republic)
patrik@bartuska.eu
www.bartuska.eu

48
Antonio Busiello (Italy)
antonio@antoniophotography.com
www.antoniophotography.com
Agent
cherry@putnam-smith.com

38
Marcello Calandrini (Italy)
bawsham54@gmail.com
www.pbase.com/bawsham/root

50
Nilanjan Das (India)
dasbappa@gmail.com
www.whisperinglades.net

24
Bridgena Barnard (South Africa)
bridgena@bridgena.co.za
www.animbo.co.za

100
Daniel Beltrá (Spain)
danielbeltra@yahoo.com
www.danielbeltra.com

65
Jordi Busqué (Spain)
info@jordibusque.com
www.jordibusque.com

142
Jack Chapman (UK)
jackpbchapman@tiscali.co.uk
http://jack.richardkchapman.co.uk
Agent
www.flpa-images.co.uk

56
Frédéric Demeuse (Belgium)
frederic.demeuse@telenet.be
Agent
http://www.naturimages.com

78
Maurizio Biancarelli (Italy)/
Wild Wonders of Europe
info@mauriziobiancarelli.net
www.mauriziobiancarelli.net
www.wild-wonders.com

58
Peter Cairns (UK)
info@northshots.com
www.northshots.com

98
Jordi Chias Pujol (Spain)
jordi@uwaterphoto.com
www.uwaterphoto.com
Agents
www.uwaterphoto.com
www.imagequestmarine.com

97
Oscar Díez (Spain)
pajaruchis@hotmail.com
www.oscardiez.es

110
Greg du Toit (South Africa)
greg@gregdutoit.com
www.gregdutoit.com

55
Ken Dyball (Australia)
africanatureimages@gmail.com
www.africanatureimages.com

52
Morkel Erasmus (South Africa)
morksnork@gmail.com
www.morkelerasmus.com

37
Yossi Eshbol (Israel)
eshbol@bezeqint.net
Agent
www.flpa-images.co.uk

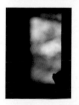

128–131
Kai Fagerström (Finland)
kai.fagerstrom@salo.fi

143
Johan Gehrisch (Sweden)
johan.gehrisch@gmail.com

75
Laurent Geslin (France)
geslin@laurent-geslin.com
www.laurent-geslin.com
Agents
www.biosphoto.com
www.naturepl.com

21
Edwin Giesbers (The Netherlands)/
Wild Wonders of Europe
info@edwingiesbers.com
www.edwingiesbers.com
www.wild-wonders.com
Agents
www.naturepl.com
www.fotonatura.com

138, 144
Fergus Gill (UK)
fergusgill@hotmail.co.uk
www.scottishnaturephotography.com

46
Axel Gomille (Germany)
axel.gomille@web.de
www.axelgomille.com

94
Juan Jesús González Ahumada
(Spain)
ahumada585@hotmail.com
www.fotonatura.org/galerias/5451/

146
Martin Gregus Jr. (Canada/Slovakia)
matkojr@shaw.ca
www.matkopictures.com

90
Eirik Grønningsæter (Norway)
eg@wildnature.no
www.wildnature.no
Agents
www.alamy.com
www.fotofil.no
www.fotonatura.com

71
Orsolya Haarberg
(Hungary)
orsolya.haarberg@freemail.hu
www.haarbergphoto.com
Agents
www.scanpix.no
www.naturepl.com

102
Thomas Haider (Austria)
thomas.haider@meduniwien.ac.at
www.thomashaider.at
Agent
www.osf.co.uk

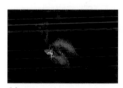

44
David Herasimtschuk (USA)
davidherasim@gmail.com
http://web.mac.com/
davidherasimtschuk/

53
Britta Jaschinski (Germany)
info@brittaphotography.com
www.brittaphotography.com

153
Will Jenkins (UK)
sjhowling@yahoo.co.uk

32
Arto Juvonen (Finland)
arto@birdphoto.fi
www.birdphoto.fi

104
Sandesh Kadur (India)
kadur.sandesh@gmail.com
www.felis.in

62
Georg Kantioler (Italy)
georg@kantioler.it
www.kantioler.it

40
Pascal Kobeh (France)
pkobeh@club-internet.fr
www.scuba-photos.com

87
Marcelo Krause (Brazil)
marcelo@underwater.com.br
www.marcelokrause.com

155
Russell T. Laman (USA)
office@timlaman.com

19, 109
Tim Laman (USA)
tim@timlaman.com
www.timlaman.com
Agents
akeating@ngs.org
www.naturepl.com

26
Jean-Michel Lenoir (France)
jm.lenoir@wanadoo.fr
www.jean-michel-lenoir.com

116–121
Mark Leong (USA)
lmrk@aol.com
Agent
www.reduxpictures.com

60
Chris Linder (USA)
chris@chrislinder.com
www.chrislinder.com

51
Esa Mälkönen (Finland)
esa.malkonen@luukku.com
www.malkonen.fi

96
Roy Mangersnes (Norway)
roy@wildphoto.no
www.wildphoto.no
Agent
www.naturepl.com

154
Lucas Marsalle (France)
jean-francois.marsalle@orange.fr

14, 132–137
Bence Máté (Hungary)
bence@matebence.hu
www.matebence.hu

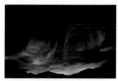

82
Kent Miklenda (Australia)
xenomundi@bigpond.com
www.kentmiklenda.com

16, 23, 61, 64
Francisco Mingorance (Spain)
jfmingorance@terra.es
www.franciscomingorance.com

34
Jim Neiger (USA)
jimn@cfl.rr.com
www.flightschoolphotography.com

76
Michael Patrick O'Neill (USA/Brazil)
mpo@msn.com
www.mpostock.com
Agents
www.nhpa.co.uk
www.oceanwideimages.com
www.seapics.com
www.photoresearchers.com
www.alamy.com

74
Chris O'Reilly (UK)
info@cornaturephotography.co.uk
www.cornaturephotography.co.uk
Agents
www.naturepl.com
www.rspb-images.co.uk

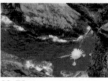

20, 72
Andrew Parkinson (UK)
andy@andrewparkinson.com
www.andrewparkinson.com
Agents
www.gettyimages.com
www.corbis.com
www.naturepl.com
www.rspb-images.com
www.flpa-images.co.uk
www.lonelyplanetimages.com
www.nhpa.co.uk
www.fotonatura.com

152
Malte Parmo (Denmark)
mail@parmo.org
www.parmo.org

150
Haijun Pei (China)
peihaijun1112@yahoo.cn

114
Jari Peltomäki (Finland)/
Wild Wonders of Europe
jari@finnature.fi
www.finnature.fi
www.wild-wonders.com
Agents
www.birdphoto.fi
www.leuku.fi
www.agami.nl
www.blickwinkel.de
www.photoshot.com

95
Thomas P. Peschak
(South Africa/Germany)
tpeschak@iafrica.com
www.thomaspeschak.com

81
Verena Popp-Hackner (Austria)
office@popphackner.com
www.popphackner.com

77
Olivier Puccia (France)
olivierpuccia@gmail.com

92
Reto Puppetti (Switzerland)
reto@shangri-la.ch
www.shangri-la.ch

112
Tomasz Raczyński (Poland)
rakus@o2.pl

86
Michel Roggo (Switzerland)
info@roggo.ch
www.roggo.ch
Agent
www.naturepl.com

30
Jürgen Ross (Germany)
juergen_ross@yahoo.de
www.naturfoto-ross.de

106
Andy Rouse (UK)
andyrouse@mac.com
www.andyrouse.net
Agent
www.naturepl.com

105
Joel Sartore (USA)
sartore@inebraska.com
www.joelsartore.com

54
Tom Schandy (Norway)
tschandy@online.no
www.tomschandy.no
Agents
www.samfoto.no
www.naturepl.com

66
Jochen Schlenker (Germany)
jochen.sc@gmail.com
www.masterfile.com

31
Andrew Schoeman (South Africa)
andrew.schoeman@andbeyond.com

42
Florian Schulz (Germany)
florian@visionsofthewild.com
www.visionsofthewild.com
Agent
Emil Herrera
emil@visionsofthewild.com

36
Ilia Shalamaev (Israel)
ilia@focuswildlife.com
www.focuswildlife.com

103, 122–127
Brian Skerry (USA)
brian@brianskerry.com
www.brianskerry.com
Agent
www.nationalgeographic.com/
imagesales

22
Tanguy Stoecklé (France)
tanguy.stoeckle@gcprovence.org
www.tanguystoeckle.fr

73
Mac Stone (USA)
macstonephoto@gmail.com
www.macstonePhoto.com

145
Ilari Miikka Kalevi Tuupanen
(Finland)
ilari.tuupanen@hotmail.com
www.ilarituupanen.net

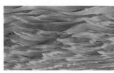

83
Floris van Breugel
(USA/The Netherlands)
floris@artinnaturephotography.com
www.artinnaturephotography.com

70
Pierre Vernay (France)
vernay92@free.fr
www.pierre-vernay.com

149
Arthur-Coriolan Wilmotte (France)
photosfaune@gmail.com
http://photosfaune.over-blog.com

101
Steve Winter (USA)
stevewinterphoto@mac.com
www.stevewinterphoto.com

84, 113
Tony Wu (USA)
tony@tony-wu.com
www.tonywublog.com

80
Kah Kit Yoong (Australia)
kahkityoong@hotmail.com
www.magichourtravelscapes.com

39
Christian Ziegler (Germany)
zieglerphoto@yahoo.com
www.naturphoto.de